GOUT DIET COOKBOOK

by Danielle De Mayo

TABLE OF CONTENT

table of content

table of content

table of content

GOUT DIET COOKBOOK

What is Gout?

Gout describes a set of conditions with one common feature – the accumulation of uric acid inside the joints.

Uric acid is a product of the catabolic reaction of purine nucleotides, and it is a standard component of urine.

Generally speaking, gout affects the joints of the feet and hands, causing edema (i.e., swelling), pain, and reduced range of motion.
According to reports, gout affects 3.9% of the population in the United States; this translates to approximately 9.2 million people. (1)

The causes of gout

Gout stems from the buildup of uric acid in the bloodstream, which eventually leads to the leakage of this chemical into the joint capsules. (2) As a result, an inflammatory reaction sets in, producing the classic signs and symptoms of gout.

Researchers identified metabolic disorders, dehydration, and certain vascular diseases as potential triggers of uric acid accumulation. Additionally, medical conditions that affect the kidneys and thyroid also interfere with the body's ability to remove excess uric acid from the blood.

Other risk factors of gout include: (3)

Age – middle-aged men and postmenopausal women
Family history – having family members with gout increases the risk
Alcohol abuse – excessive alcohol consumption precipitates gout
Medication – diuretics, cyclosporine
Concurrent medical conditions – high blood pressure, thyroid disease, diabetes, kidney disease, and obstructive sleep apnea
Dietary choices – foods rich in gout-producing purines (e.g., some fish, organ meats, game meats)

The signs and symptoms of gout

Acute gout attacks present with a variety of symptoms that last between 3 to 10 days.

Classic symptoms include:
Pain
Edema
The warmth of the skin above the joint

Once the attack subsides, you will not experience any of these symptoms. Unfortunately, untreated gout can become chronic, especially when the triggering factor is still present. Moreover, hard lumps (i.e., tophi) can deposit around the skin, joints, and soft tissues, which permanently damages the structure of your joints. (4)

After pain treatment, to provide relief, the first therapy goal is to lower the levels of uric acids in the blood, which allows preventing new painful episodes (or at least a reduction in their frequency).

A careful and mindful diet can help reduce uric acid levels in the blood, and while it cannot be called a cure, it can effectively reduce the risk of recurrent gout attacks and slow the progression of joint damage. Parallel to the pharmacological intervention of medical relevance, the diet must be customized according to the patient's needs.

What kind of food is good and which to avoid

Nutrition plays a vital role in both the prevention and treatment of gout; for example, alcohol abuse or a diet that is too rich and careless often increases uric acids.

Foods that can trigger gout attacks

If you are susceptible to gout attacks, you need to avoid purine-producing foods. These foods typically contain more than 200 mg of purine per 3.5 ounces.

Here is a list of the significant purine-producing foods to avoid:

Fish: Herring, trout, mackerel, tuna, sardines, anchovies, haddock
Other seafood: Scallops, crab, shrimp, and roe
Organ meats: These include liver, kidneys, sweetbreads, and brain
Game meats: Examples include pheasant, veal, and venison, fatty meat broth or meat extracts, sausage, goose, duck, lard
Sugary beverages: Especially fruit juices and sugary sodas
Added sugars: honey, agave nectar, and high-fructose corn syrup
Yeasts: Nutritional yeast, brewer's yeast, and other yeast supplements
Alcohol specialty beer

A too restrictive diet also leads to a rise in uric acid concentration, derived from particular molecules' metabolism, called purines.

If you are overweight or obese, your diet should be moderately low-calorie to reach the desired weight gradually, but not excessively drastic to avoid causing a further increase in blood uric acid levels.

The general advice, beyond these first indications, are

Avoid prolonged fasting.
Avoid a diet too rich in fats and proteins, consequently avoiding or decreasing foods rich in purines (anchovies, brain, liver, kidneys, shrimp, sardines, ...).
Avoid alcohol consumption.
Drink plenty of water to prevent kidney stones from forming.
Consume copious amounts of fruits, vegetables, and whole grains, which provide healthy carbohydrates in complex form.

Following foods are good foods for GOUT diet:
plant foods: fruit, vegetables, nuts, seeds, including cereals, lean fish, chicken, turkey, skimmed milk, extra virgin olive oil, coffee, tea, and herbal teas.

Foods to consume with moderation:
mayonnaise, asparagus, peas, tomatoes, and spinach (limit to use these vegetables because of the suspect of relationship with the possibility of developing kidney stones, but a good intake of water allows their consumption), pork or beef (lean parts only), whole milk, dried fruit, simple sugars.

Another important trick is not to use too much fat when cooking, preferring approaches such as: steaming, boiling, plate, foil, sautéed.

If you want to consume a fry, you need to make sure that the oil temperature is high enough not to be absorbed by the food, but obviously, avoid fried foods in recent remission of an acute attack.

Instead of salt, use: garlic, onion, various spices, vinegar, lemon.

How to relieve your gout pain with food - homemade remedies

In this section, we will tackle some of the foods that improve the symptoms of gout.

Ginger
Researchers found that applying ginger to the joints can relieve pain induced by gout.
(5)
In one laboratory study, researchers analyzed the effects of ginger supplementation on uric acid levels. The results showed that regular intake of ginger prevents hyperuricemia (i.e., elevated levels of uric acid in the blood). (6)

Here is what you need to do to apply ginger on the affected articulations:
Turn ginger into a paste by boiling water with one tablespoon of grated fresh ginger root
Soak a washcloth in the mixture
When it cools down, apply the washcloth to the affected joints for 15–30 minutes.
Do this at least once a day.

Cherries
According to one study, cherries (e.g., sour, sweet, red, black) effectively dampen inflammation induced by gout attacks. (7)
Researchers believe that cherries exert their anti-inflammatory and antioxidative effects, translating into pain relief and reduced swelling.

Magnesium
Low magnesium levels can often exacerbate gout attacks and similar conditions.
In a 2015 study, scientists found a correlation between adequate magnesium consumption and lower uric acid levels. Interestingly, these findings were only noted in men and not women. (8)

Nettle tea
Stinging nettle (Urtica dioica) is a potent remedy that addresses inflammation and pain.
In one study, nettle tea showed kidney-protecting properties that improve the clearance of uric acid. (9)
To prepare this tea, steep two tablespoons of dried nettle in some water and boil it.

Milk thistle seeds

Milk thistle improves the function of the liver and kidneys.
In one study, researchers found that this herb reduces uric acid levels even when patients have kidney failure. (10)

Hibiscus

Hibiscus is a traditional herb used as food, tea, or garden flower.
Adding hibiscus in a home remedy can relieve symptoms of gout by lowering the levels of uric acid. (11)

References

1-Singh, G., Lingala, B., & Mithal, A. (2019). Gout and hyperuricemia in the USA: prevalence and trends. Rheumatology (Oxford, England), 58(12), 2177–2180. https://doi.org/10.1093/rheumatology/kez196

2-Ragab, G., Elshahaly, M., & Bardin, T. (2017). Gout: An old disease in a new perspective-A review. Journal of advanced research, 8(5), 495-511.

3-Singh, J. A., Reddy, S. G., & Kundukulam, J. (2011). Risk factors for gout and prevention: a systematic review of the literature. Current opinion in rheumatology, 23(2), 192.

4-Ragab, G., Elshahaly, M., & Bardin, T. (2017). Gout: An old disease in a new perspective-A review. Journal of advanced research, 8(5), 495-511.

5-https://www.ijstr.org/final-print/oct2017/Effect-Of-Red-Ginger-Compress-To-Decrease-Scale-Of-Pain-Gout-Arthiris-Patients.pdf

6-http://www.journalijar.com/uploads/666_IJAR-7458.pdf

7-Singh, J. A., Bharat, A., & Edwards, N. L. (2015). An internet survey of common treatments used by patients with gout, including cherry extract and juice and other dietary supplements. Journal of clinical rheumatology: practical reports on rheumatic & musculoskeletal diseases, 21(4), 225.

8-Wang, Y. L., Zeng, C., Wei, J., Yang, T., Li, H., Deng, Z. H., ... & Lei, G. H. (2015). Association between dietary magnesium intake and hyperuricemia. PLoS One, 10(11), e0141079.

9-Salih, N. A. (2015). Effect of nettle (Urtica dioica) extracts on gentamicin-induced nephrotoxicity in male rabbits. Asian Pacific Journal of Tropical Biomedicine, 5(9), 756-760.

10-Karakuş, A., Değer, Y., & Yıldırım, S. (2017). Protective effect of Silybum marianum and Taraxacum officinale extracts against oxidative kidney injuries induced by carbon tetrachloride in rats. Renal failure, 39(1), 1-6.

11-Kuo, C. Y., Kao, E. S., Chan, K. C., Lee, H. J., Huang, T. F., & Wang, C. J. (2012). Hibiscus sabdariffa L. extracts reduce serum uric acid levels in oxonate-induced rats. Journal of Functional Foods, 4(1), 375-381.

TABLE

Food with moderate purine mg/100g

Beef chuck, filet, fore rib, entrecote, shoulder, roast beef	120
Bean dry white seed	128
soya dry seed dry	190
chicken breast	175
chicken for roasting	115
chicken legs with skin and bone	110
fish anchovy	239
fish cod	109
fish haddock	139
fish herring roe	190
fish mackerel	145
fish redfish	241
fish salmon	170
fish sole	131
fish eel smoked	78
crayfish	60
ham cooked	131
grape dried raisin	107
lentil dry seed	127
linseed	105
lobster	118
peas chick, dry garbanzo seed	109
poppy seed	170
rabbit meat average	132

Food with low purine mg/100gr

almond	37	corn sweet	52
apple	14	cress	28
apricot	73	crispbread	60
asparagus	23	cucumber	7
aubergine	21	currant red	17
avocado	19	date dried	35
banana	57	elderberry black	33
bean sprouts	80	endive	17
bean french string beans haricot	37	fenel leaves	14
beans french dried	45	fig dried	64
blueberry, huckleberry, bilberry	22	grape	27
bread white	14	kale	48
broccoli	81	kiwi	18
brussels sprouts	69	leek	74
cabbage red savoy	35	lettuce	13
cabbage white	22	lettuce lambs	38
carrot	17	melon cantelope	33
cauliflower	51	mushroom chanterelle	17
celeriac	30	nuts brazil	23
cheese brie	7	nuts hazelnut	37
cheese cheddar ceshire	6	nuts peanut	79
cheese cottage	9	nuts walnut	25
cheese edam	7	oats whole grain	94
cheese Limburger	32	olive marinated green	29
cherry morelly	18	onion	13
cherry sweet	7	orange	19
chicory	12	parsley leaf	57
Chinese leaves	21	pasta made with eggs	40
chives	67	pea pod and seed, green	84

Food with low purine mg/100gr

pea seed dry	95
peach	21
pear	12
peppers green	55
pineapple	19
plum	24
plum dried	64
potato	16
potato cooked with skin	18
pumpkin	44
radish	15
radishes	14
raspberry	18
rhubarb	12
rice white	26
rols bread	21
sauerkraut dripped off	16
sesame seeds	62
spinach	57
strawberry	21
tomato	11
yogurt 3.5 %fat	8

Reference: https://elevatehealthaz.com/wp-content/Purine%20Table.pdf

Many recipes in this cookbook mention using vegetable broth or vegetable soup. Here is the recipe for healthy vegetable broth with very low sodium.

VEGETABLE BROTH

Ingredients:

2 onions chopped

4 cloves garlic

3 carrots

4 celery stalks

5 sprigs of fresh thyme

1 bay leaf

1 small bunch of fresh parsley

½ small bunch of fresh basil leaf

1 tsp black peppercorns

1 medium leek (especially the green parts),

1 fennel,

1 tomato,

1 small bunch of fresh parsnip,

1 tbsp olive oil

Preparation:

Wash all vegetables. In a big pot, warm olive oil, add onions, and stir for 2 minutes. Add all coarsely chopped vegetables and spices. Add water to cover vegetables and bring to a boil. When boiling, reduce the temperature to medium and simmer for 1 hour. Let it cool for a while, and then drain the vegetables. You can use the vegetable soup clean and freeze it for later. If you want, you can blend all vegetables into the vegetable soup and freeze the smoothie soup in small glasses or ice cubes. The broth will have a mild taste if you add more water, depending on you. You can add or change any vegetable from the ingredients list but avoid potatoes and other starchy ones, zucchini, aubergine, and beans. You can roast the vegetables in the oven for one hour before using them as described in the recipe. Roast just hard vegetables, let the leaves boil, and the soup will be even more aromatic.

VEGETABLES

SALADS

SPICY PLANTAINS

Ingredients:

2 firm-ripe plantains - a yellow one
2 spring onions finely chopped
1 fresh tomato chopped
1 red pepper thinly sliced
½ tsp of mild curry powder
1 tbsp rapeseed oil
the small stem of ginger about a
tbsp peeled and finely chopped
scotch bonnet pepper to taste
approx 8 mg purine

Instructions:

Make an incision along the length
of each plantain so it is easier to
peel once cooked. Boil in water for
10-15 minutes until plantain can
be easily pierced with a fork.
Remove from water and leave to
cool.

Heat the rapeseed oil in a large
non-stick pan. Add the spring
onion, red pepper, ginger, and
tomato and cook gently for 8-10
minutes—season with black
pepper to taste. Meanwhile, peel
the plantains, discard the skin, and
slice into discs about 1 inch thick.
Transfer plantains to the pan and
mix well. Serve as a starchy food
with meat or fish and a portion of
vegetables.

SPICY BANANA BREAD

Ingredients:

3 ripe bananas - mashed
2 medium eggs
1 tsp baking powder
3 tsp mixed spice
1 tsp vanilla essence
3 tbsp caster sugar
¾ cup plain white flour
5 tbsp oats
approx 1,5 mg purine

Instructions:

Combine the eggs, spices, and banana in a large bowl and mix well. Sieve the flour and fold into the mixture, then add the oats. Use fry light or vegetable oil to grease a baking tin or line with greaseproof paper. Pour in the mixture and level the surface. Bake in the middle of the oven at 190 C/370 F for 34 - 40 minutes. Allow the bread to cool for 15 minutes and turn out onto a wire rack. Serve warm.

Servings: 8

Calories: 240

ready in 5 min

POPPYSEED SALAD

Ingredients:

Lettuce
Onion green
string beans
Acai berry
Citrus fruits
Grapes with no seeds
Avocado

For Dressing:
vinaigrette
3 tbsp of poppy seeds
Olive oil
salt pepper
approx 12 mg purine

Instructions:

Rinse the string beans. Wash and clean vegetables, cut onion green, lettuce, and avocado.
Mix all ingredients in a bowl.
Add two or three tbsps of dressing, and toss.

Servings: 4

Calories: 56

ready in 10min

SEAWEED SALAD

Ingredients:

2 tbsp grams white sesame seeds
1 cup grams fresh wakame seaweed
1 tbsp Lime juice
1 tsp of sugar
chili's (freshly ground)
2 tbsp sesame seed oil
approx 7 mg purine

Instructions:

In a dry skillet, toast sesame seeds until fragrant and light brown. Remove the skillet from the heat and set it aside to cool. Drain the seaweed after rinsing it.

Add the seaweed to a bowl with lime juice, sugar, and pepper. Mix the sesame seeds and oil, season with salt and pepper to taste, and serve.

Servings: 4

Calories: 348

ready in 25min

BREAD SALAD

Ingredients:

6 whole-grain baguette slices
3 tbsp olive oil
2 shallots
one garlic clove
2 tbsp pitted black olives
1 basil bunch
1 tbsp vinegar (white)
1 cup feta cheese
cayenne
 approx 13 mg purine

Instructions:

Cut the whole grain baguette into 1-inch cubes with a sharp knife. Heat 1 tbsp olive oil in a skillet and toast the bread cubes for 5 minutes over medium heat. Put them aside. Peel the shallots and garlic cloves. Chop the garlic and cut the shallots into fine circles. Cut the olives in half. Basil should be washed, dried, and finely chopped. Combine the prepared ingredients and the bread cubes in a mixing bowl, add remaining oil, pepper, vinegar, and crumble the feta on top.
Serve the bread salad with olives on four plates.

Servings: 4

Calories: 256

ready in 25min

SPRING SALAD

Ingredients:

3 cups mixed salad (for example, loose-leaf lettuce, butterhead lettuce, Batavia, and radicchio)
1 onion
3 tbsp white wine vinegar,
4 tbsp extra virgin olive oil
chilies
half cup parmesan cheese (a piece)
daisies (to serve)
approx 12 mg purine

Instructions:

Wash the salad leaves, sort them, shake them dry, and cut them into bite-size bits. Peel the onion and thinly slice or dice.
Combine vinegar and olive oil in a salad dressing shaker. Shake well. Add pepper to taste.
Mix the salad leaves with the onion and divide evenly among four plates. Sprinkle each dish with salad dressing. Serve the salad with shredded Parmesan and daisies sprinkled on top.

Servings: 4

Calories: 200

ready in 35min

PAPAYA SALAD

Ingredients:

1 ½ cup salsify
2 tbsp apple cider vinegar
1 ½ cup papaya (1 papaya)
1 chicory
½ cup radicchio
½ cup gorgonzola (45% fat in dry matter)
½ cup yogurt (3.5% fat)
1 tbsp olive oil
pepper
4 tbsp grainy oat flakes
1 handful basil (5 g)
approx 27 mg purine

Instructions:

Thoroughly clean salsify, peel and cut into pieces approx. 1 inch in size. Boil them in salted water with 1 tbsp of apple cider vinegar for 15 minutes. Then drain, rinse with cold water, and set aside.

In the meantime, peel and core the papaya and cut it into fine strips. Wash and clean the chicory and radicchio and cut them into fine strips.

Put the Gorgonzola with yogurt, olive oil, and 1 tbsp apple cider vinegar in a tall container and puree finely with a hand blender, adding a little water if necessary. Season to taste with salt and pepper.

Roast the oatmeal in a hot pan without fat over medium heat for 3-4 minutes. Wash the basil, shake dry and cut into fine strips.

Arrange salsify, papaya, chicory, and radicchio on four plates, pour the dressing over them and sprinkle with oat flakes and basil strips

STRAWBERRY DRESSING SALAD

Ingredients:

3 eggs
½ cup of lamb's lettuce
1 cup cucumber
radish bunch
12 spring onions, fretted
½ cup strawberries (or other seasonally available fruit)
2 tbsp olive oil
1 tbsp balsamic vinaigrette
salt, cayenne
thyme, dried
½ cup Sheep cheese (45 percent fat in dry matter)
2 pcs whole grain bread
approx 15 mg purine

Instructions:

Boil eggs for about 6 minutes, then set aside to cool.

Clean, wash and spin dry the lamb's lettuce. Cucumber, radishes, and spring onions should be cleaned, washed, and sliced. Strawberries should be cleaned and washed before being cut into fine cubes.

Combine the strawberries, olive oil, and vinegar in a mixing bowl—season to taste with salt, pepper, and thyme.

Peel and cut the eggs in half.

Crumble the sheep's cheese.

Combine the lettuce, cucumber, radish slices, spring onions, and feta cheese in a salad bowl. Serve the salad with the eggs on top, drizzled with the dressing, and bread on the side.

SALAD WITH FLOWERS

Ingredients:

4 cups spring greens (mixed)
(arugula, sorrel, young dandelion,
watercress, etc.)
1 3/4 cup cheese, diced (cheddar,
pepper jack, gouda; may substitute
cheese of your choosing)
2 tbsp. vinegar (fruit)
1 tbsp lemon
5 tbsp. extra virgin olive oil
Black pepper freshly ground
blossoms that are edible (such as
pansies; dandelions, and daisies)
approx 19 mg purine

Instructions:

Clean, wash and rinse the mixed
greens. Divide them into four salad
bowls, and sprinkle diced cheese
over the top of each salad bowl.
Whisk the vinegar, lemon juice, oil,
salt, and pepper in a small mixing
bowl until well combined. Drizzle
over salad and add new edible
flowers for a finishing touch.

Servings: 4

Calories: 166

ready in 40min

FRESH SUMMER SALAD

Ingredients:

4 cups white asparagus (trimmed)
a pot of hot water
1 tsp butter
2 lemons (juice)
2 2/3 cup strawberries, chopped
3 tbsp balsamic vinegar (white)
2 tbsp olive oil (extra virgin)
2 tbsp lemon juice
peppers, freshly ground
as finishing touch, basil (herb)
arugula
approx 18 mg purine

Instructions:

Cut the ends off the asparagus
stalks and peel them.
Boil water with asparagus, butter,
and lemon juice until soft
asparagus. Drain the asparagus
and rinse it in cold water before
draining it again.
Chop the asparagus coarsely and
combine it with the strawberries.
Combine the vinegar, oil, lemon
juice, salt, and pepper to taste in a
mixing bowl.
Mix the asparagus and
strawberries with the dressing,
divide among serving plates.
Serve with basil and rocket on the
side.

Servings: 4

Calories: 383

ready in 35min

STRAWBERRY LENTIL SALAD

Ingredients:

1 cup lentils

1 cup edamame

2 rhubarb sticks (young)

1 cup strawberries,

1 cup Snow peas,

1 tbsp sesame seed oil

2 tbsp lemon juice

bunch of basil

½ cup bocconcini (small fresh mozzarella balls)

approx 90 mg purine

Instructions:

Boil the lentils until they are soft, as directed on the packet. Drain, set it aside, and let it cool.

Boil the edamame for 5 minutes in salted water. Drain and cool before removing the edamame from the pods.

Prepare the rhubarb and strawberries by washing, cleaning, and slicing them. Snow peas should be washed, cleaned, and cut in half diagonally.

Combine sesame oil, lemon juice, salt, and pepper in a large mixing bowl. Basil should be washed, dried, and coarsely chopped.

Add all ingredients together with the dressing and divide among four bowls. Distribute the mozzarella among the bowls.

Servings: 4

Calories: 130

ready in 40min

PIGEON PEAS SALAD

Ingredients:

2 cups green pigeon peas
1 cup of sweetcorn in unsalted water drained
2 medium carrots peeled and grated
2 spring onions finely chopped

for the sauce:
3 tbsp olive oil
1 tbsp balsamic vinegar
1 tiny chili seeds removed, finely chopped
1 tsp minced garlic
juice of 1 lime
a handful of parsley roughly chopped
approx 58 mg purine

Instructions:

Use dried peas, and boil them for about 30 minutes. Drain and leave to cool.
If you use canned peas: empty the contents into a colander. Rinse with cold water and drain well.
Combine all ingredients for the dressing in a large bowl, and season with black pepper to taste. Pour the sauce over the peas, sweet corn, and grated carrot, mixing well. Add chopped spring onions to garnish.

AVOCADO AND PAPAYA SALAD

Ingredients:

4 avocado
4 papayas peeled, halved, and seeded
2 limes zested and juiced
2 baby gem lettuces
1 small red onion finely diced
1 handful of cherry tomatoes halved
1 clove garlic minced
½ tsp freshly ground black pepper
½ tsp cayenne pepper
¼ cup olive oil
approx 17 mg purine

Instructions:

Slice the avocado lengthwise into ½ inch slices. Slice the papaya widthwise into ½ inch slices, drizzle with the juice of 1 lime immediately. Arrange slices overlapping and alternating on a bed of baby gem lettuce, then add the cherry tomatoes and onions.
In a small bowl, combine remaining ingredients, mix well, spoon over the salad and serve immediately.

Servings: 4

Calories: 503

ready in 10 min

AVOCADO HARICOT SALAD

Ingredients:

Dressing:
2 tbsp olive oil
¼ cup lime juice
2 tsp cumin
2 tsp chili powder
1 tsp salt
1 tsp pepper
Salad:
¼ cup fresh cilantro, chopped
2 cups haricot beans, drained, rinsed
1 cucumber, chopped, quartered
5 cherry tomatoes halved
1 onion, chopped
1 avocado, diced
⅓ cup carrot, shredded
approx 25 mg purine

Instructions:

For the dressing: combine dressing ingredients in a small bowl. Whisk together until mixed thoroughly. Combine beans, cucumber, tomatoes, onion, avocado, carrots, and dressing in a large bowl. Toss together until evenly combined.

Servings: 4

Calories: 208

ready in 15 min

CHOPPED MEDITERRANEAN SALAD

Ingredients:

2 cucumbers
4 tomatoes
1 red onion
½ cup feta cheese
2 tbsp olive oil
2 tbsp red wine vinegar
salt,
black pepper, to taste
1 tbsp lemon juice
1 cup olive
approx 10 mg purine

Instructions:

Peel the cucumbers. Cut into discs, and then quarter the discs. Place in a large salad bowl.

Cut tomatoes into quarters, lengthwise, and then rotate and cut into large chunks. Add to the salad bowl.

Cut the red onion in half, removing the skin, stem, and bottom. Thinly slice and add to the bowl.

Add the feta cheese, olive oil, red wine vinegar, salt, pepper, lemon juice, and olives to the salad bowl and toss gently.

Servings: 5

Calories: 342

ready in 15mn

SOUTHWESTERN SALAD

Ingredients:

Dressing:
1 avocado, halved
1 clove garlic
½ tsp salt
½ tsp pepper
2 tbsp olive oil
1 tbsp fresh cilantro
1 lime, juiced
Salad:
1 head lettuce, chopped
1 cup bell pepper, chopped
¼ cup fresh cilantro
1 cup black beans
½ cup red onion, chopped
1 cup corn
¼ cup scallion
¾ cup tomato, chopped
approx 18 mg purine

Instructions:

Add all dressing ingredients to a
blender, blend until smooth.
Add lettuce, peppers, cilantro,
beans, onion, corn, green onion,
and tomatoes in a large bowl.
Top with prepared dressing; toss.

Servings: 4

Calories: 250

ready in 15 min

LOW-CARB CHICKEN SALAD

Ingredients:

⅔ cup greek yogurt low fat
1 tbsp lime juice
pepper, to taste
⅛ tsp chili powder
1 avocado, cubed, divided
2 chicken breasts, cooked and
shredded
1 stalk celery, diced
2 tbsp red onion, diced
salt
bread, low-carb, for serving,
optional
fresh cilantro leaf for garnish
approx 40 mg purine

Instructions:

In a blender or food processor,
combine the yogurt, lime juice,
pepper, and chili powder, add ½ of
the avocado and blend until creamy.
Combine the chicken, yogurt sauce,
celery, the remaining ½ avocado,
onion, and salt in a medium bowl.
Mix until well combined.
Serve on the low-carb bread and
garnish with cilantro.

Servings: 2

Calories: 161

ready in 15 min

AVOCADO AND TOMATO SALAD

Ingredients:

1 avocado, diced

1 cup cherry tomato, finely chopped

¼ medium red onion, thinly sliced

½ lime, juiced

salt, to taste

2 tbsps fresh parsley, chopped

bunch of cashews

approx 20 mg purine

Instructions:

Combine all ingredients in a bowl and gently stir.

Servings: 6

Calories: 170

ready in 15min

EGGS WITH VEGETABLE

Ingredients:

8 large eggs
1/2 yellow onion chopped
1/2 cup carrots chunk chopped and steamed
1/4 cup green peas
1/2 cup green bell pepper chopped
1/4 cup bean sprouts cut in half
1 tbsp light soy sauce
3 tbsp sesame oil divided
approx 46 mg purine

Instructions:

Add the eggs, onion, carrots, peas, bell pepper, bean sprouts, and soy sauce together in a bowl and whisk to combine.

In a large skillet, heat 1 tsp of sesame oil at a time for each pancake you fry on medium heat.

Add about 1/3 cup of mixture per pancake and fry for 3-4 minutes on the first one and 1-2 minutes on the other side

Servings: 2

Calories: 581

ready in 15min

ZUCCHINI OMELETTE

Ingredients:

1 cup - one large zucchini
2 red onions
1 red pepper
6 eggs
1 cup milk (1.5 percent fat)
cumin
paprika powder
2 tbsp of extra virgin olive oil
½ cup soft goat cheese (45 percent fat in dry matter)
½ cup arugula
approx 30 mg purine

Instructions:

Clean and wash the zucchini, halved lengthwise, and cut into slices. Peel and halve the onions and cut them into strips. Halve, core, wash and cut the pepper into strips.

Whisk eggs with milk, season with salt, pepper, and paprika powder. Heat 1 tbsp of oil in a pan and fry half of the vegetables for about 5 minutes. Add half of the egg-milk and let it set. Fry a second a omelet the same way.

Cut the cheese into slices. Wash the rocket and shake dry. Spread the goat cheese and rocket on the omelets, slide out of the pan and serve.

Servings: 4

Calories: 304

ready in 25 min

OMELETTE WITH MUSHROOMS

Ingredients:

1 cup brown mushrooms
1 shallot
2 tbsps of extra virgin olive oil
cumin
8 eggs
half cup milk (1.5 percent fat)
1 pinch turmeric powder
3 slices cheddar cheese
half bunch chervil
approx 28 mg purine

Instructions:

Clean the mushrooms and cut them into slices. Peel and finely dice shallots. Heat 1 tbsp of olive oil in a pan. Add mushrooms and shallots and sauté for 3–4 minutes over medium heat. Season with salt and pepper, remove from the pan, and set aside. Whisk eggs with milk—season with one pinch of turmeric, salt, and pepper. Brush a coated pan with a bit of oil, add 1/4 of the egg mixture and swirl to distribute it evenly. Top with 1/4 of the fried mushrooms. Cook the omelet over medium heat for 2-3 minutes and brown lightly. Pluck 1/4 of the Cheddar into pieces, cover the omelet with it, slide out of the pan and keep warm in the preheated oven at 80 ° C / 170 F. Bake three more omelets in the same way. Wash the chervil, shake dry and pluck the leaves. Garnish each omelet with pepper and chervil tips and serve.

Servings: 4

Calories: 280

ready in 20 min

SIMPLY OMELET

Ingredients:

1 tbsp olive oil (plus more for the omelets)
½ cup bell pepper
½ cup sliced cremini or button mushrooms
½ cup diced onion
taste with black pepper and salt
8 eggs
2 tbsp milk (low fat)
½ cup sharp shredded Cheddar
approx 28 mg purine

Instructions:

In a medium sauté pan, heat the olive oil on medium. Add onion and mushrooms and fry for 7 minutes, until the bell pepper, mushrooms, and onions are softened and lightly browned. Season with salt and pepper
In a mixing bowl, whisk together the eggs and milk until smooth.
In a small non-stick skillet, heat the oil over medium-high heat.
Pour one-quarter of the eggs into the pan and, as soon as they start to set, scrape the egg from the bottom with a wooden spoon, working from one hand to the other (like you were scrambling eggs). When the egg is almost over, stop scraping and scatter a quarter of the cheese and a quarter of the vegetable mixture around the omelet. Fold the egg over on itself with a spatula. Transfer the omelet to a warm plate by sliding it out of the pan. Create four omelets this way.

Servings: 6　　　　　　Calories: 170　　　　　　ready in 15min

SALAD OMELETTE WRAP

Ingredients:

4 lettuce leaves
½ cup Carrots,
Black pepper, freshly ground

The omelet's Ingredients
4 eggs
2 tbsp butter
approx 18 mg purine

Instructions:

Wash the lettuce leaves and cut them into thin strips after draining them. Carrots should be peeled and sliced thinly.

In a mixing bowl, beat the eggs. In an 8-inch (20-cm) skillet, melt one tbsp of butter and add half of the egg mixture. Remove the omelet from the skillet until the egg has set, and repeat with the remaining egg.

To make a wrap, place the omelets on a tray, top with lettuce strips and carrots, season with salt and pepper, and roll-up.

Serve by slicing in half on the diagonal.

42

Servings: 4

Calories: 320

ready in 40min

TURMERIC PANCAKES AND LEEK

Ingredients:

½ cup wholemeal spelled flour

1 cup milk

2 eggs

salt

1 tsp turmeric powder

1 cup leek (1 small stick)

1 zucchini

1 apple

3 tbsp rapeseed oil

½ cup cream cheese (45% fat in dry matter)

pepper

¼ tsp ground caraway seeds

¼ tsp dried marjoram

approx 28 mg purine

Instructions:

Mix flour with milk, eggs, 2–4 tbsps of water, salt, and turmeric powder to form a smooth dough and leave to swell for 10 minutes. In the meantime, clean and wash the leek and courgette and cut them into thin rings and pieces. Wash the apple, cut in half, core, and cut into small pieces.

Heat 1 tbsp of oil in a pan. Sauté the leek and zucchini in it over medium heat for 5 minutes. Add apple and sauté for 3 minutes. Add the cream cheese and 3–4 tbsps of water and stir until creamy. Season with salt, pepper, caraway seeds, and marjoram.

For the pancakes, spread a large pan with 1 tsp of oil each. Pour in 1 ladle of the egg mix and fry on medium heat for 2-3 minutes on each side. Fill the pancakes with vegetables and serve.

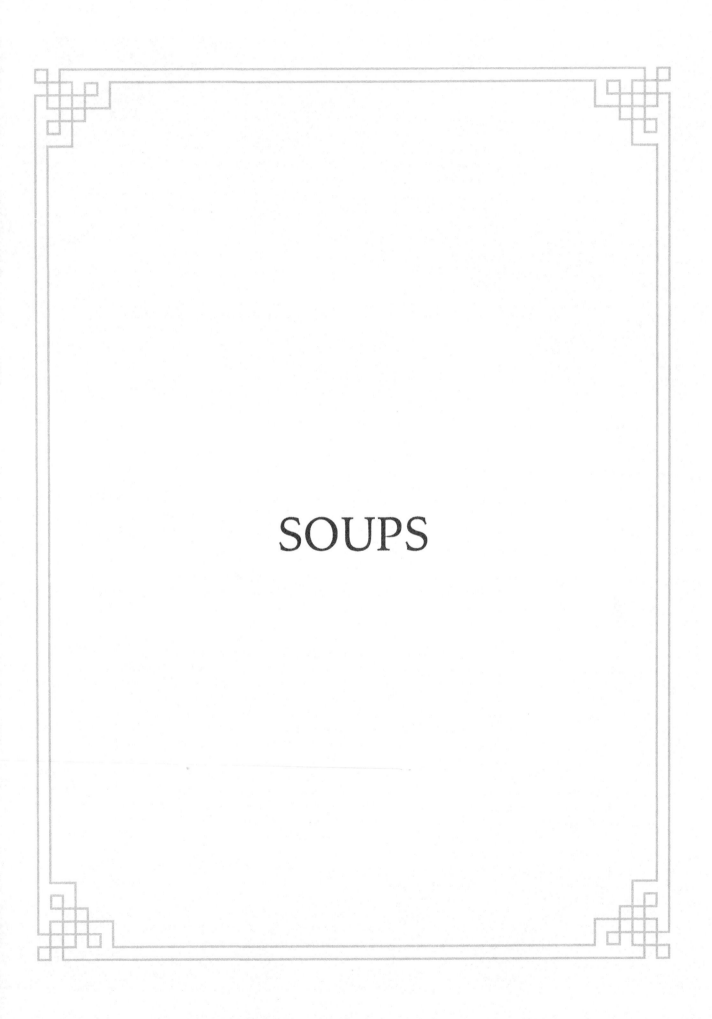

SOUPS

Servings: 6

Calories: 205

ready in 1 hour

MINESTRONE-VEGETABLE SOUP

Ingredients:

5 tbsp extra virgin olive oil
1 white onion, finely chopped
1 garlic clove, finely chopped
2 peeled and cubed potatoes (or sweet potatoes)
1 cup peeled and cubed pumpkin
2 thickly cut carrots
1 thickly cut celery stalk
1 small head of broccoli, cut into small pieces
1 cubed zucchini
1 finely chopped leek
1 cup peas (frozen)
Water (1.5 liters) (or vegetable stock)
1 cup vegetable broth
a handful of vermicelli rice (or another small pasta shape)
black pepper, freshly ground
a few finely chopped new basil leaves
Grated Parmesan cheese is an optional topping.
approx 28 mg purine

Instructions:

Heat the extra virgin olive oil in a large pot over low heat, add the onion and garlic, cook for 3 minutes or until the onion is translucent.
Add all vegetables, starting with the hard ones (carrots, potatoes, pumpkin), then the softer ones (except the frozen peas), and combine well.
Boil the water, and vegetable broth, reduce to low heat and gently simmer for 30 minutes. Ten minutes before the cooking time, add the frozen peas.
Boil for another minute after adding the rice vermicelli. If using pasta, cook it in the soup until al dente (about 10 minutes) or as directed on the package.
Take the pan from the heat, season with salt and pepper, and whisk in the basil leaves. Serve in individual bowls with parmesan cheese and garlic bread.

Servings: 6

Calories: 154

ready in 1 hour

MEXICAN VEGETABLE SOUP

Ingredients:

1 1/2 cup yellow onion, chopped

1 1/2 tbsp extra virgin olive oil

2 garlic cloves, minced

5 cups vegetable broth (low sodium)

1 1/2 cans diced tomatoes with green chilies

1 3/4 cup zucchini (chopped)

Optional: 1 ¼ cup diced green beans

1 diced red bell pepper

1 tsp oregano (dried) (Mexican oregano if you have it)

1 tsp cumin powder

1 3/4 cup frozen corn or canned hominy, drained and rinsed

2 tbsp lime juice

1/2 cup cilantro, chopped

approx 38 mg purine

Instructions:

In a large pot, heat the olive oil over medium-high heat. Add the onions and carrots, cook for 3 minutes, and add garlic and cook for another minute. Season with salt and pepper, add the vegetable broth, onions, zucchini, green beans, bell pepper, oregano, and cumin. Bring to a boil, then reduce to medium-low heat, cover, and boil until the vegetables are tender, around 20 minutes.

Boil until the corn is cooked through, stirring in the lime juice and cilantro. Heat the dish before serving.

DETOX CABBAGE SOUP

Ingredients:

1/2 cabbage head
a total of 6 celery stalks
1 onion, big
1 bell pepper, green
5 cloves of garlic
Optional: 1/2 tsp red pepper flakes
1 tbsp oregano
1 cups vegetable stock
salt and pepper to taste
approx 22 mg purine

Instructions:

In a big pot over medium-high heat, warm some oil.
Fry the onions, celery, and peppers until they are translucent, around 5 minutes.
Season with salt and pepper, then add the red pepper flakes and oregano.
Add garlic and roast, constantly stirring until the garlic is fragrant.
Add the chicken stock and cabbage.
Cook until the cabbage is tender, about 15 minutes.

SPRING ASPARAGUS SOUP

Ingredients:

2 1/2 cups sliced asparagus,
2 tsp coconut butter
3 shallots, chopped
1/2 cup red potatoes, chopped
3 cups vegetable broth
8 asparagus spears (halved, for garnish)
approx 20 mg purine

Instructions:

Sauté the asparagus spears for 30 seconds in 1/2 of the coconut butter and set aside for garnish.

In a deep non-stick pan, melt the remaining coconut butter, add the shallots and potatoes and cook for 3 to 4 minutes.

Pour in 2 cups vegetable stock, stir well, and cook until the potatoes are soft. Stir in the asparagus and cook for a few minutes more. Allow cooling.

Puree the mixture in a mixer until it is smooth.

Return the puree to the pan, season with salt and pepper, and add the remaining vegetable stock. Bring to a boil.

Garnish with sautéed asparagus spears and serve immediately.

Servings: 2

Calories: 533

ready in 14min

PEA SOUP

Ingredients:

1 shallot
1 garlic clove
2 tbsp olive oil
1 cup peas (frozen)
1 cup vegetable broth
4 dill stems
½ cup feta cheese
½ cup whipped cream
Chili flakes (optional)
1 tbsp black sesame seeds
approx 50 mg purine

Instructions:

Peel the garlic and shallot. Heat 1 tbsp of oil and sauté shallots and garlic for 3 minutes over medium heat in a saucepan. Cook for another 3 minutes after adding the peas. After that, add the vegetable stock and cook for 5 minutes. Meanwhile, wash and dry the dill before plucking it into small bits. Using your hands, crumble the feta cheese.

Next, pour the cream and finely puree the soup with half of the dill using a hand blender: salt, pepper, and chili flakes to taste in the pea soup. Fill two bowls with the remaining dill, feta, and sesame seeds, and drizzle with the remaining oil.

LENTIL AND POTATO SOUP

Ingredients:

3 carrots
1 cup potatoes
2 tbsp olive oil
½ cup red lentil
2 tbsp turmeric powder
4 cups vegetable broth
1 tbsp Tomato paste
cayenne
2 tbsp whipped cream
2 slices wholemeal sourdough bread
1 handful basil fresh
approx 50 mg purine

Instructions:

Peel and cut the carrots and potatoes into small cubes after cleaning them.
In a saucepan, heat 1 tbsp of oil for 4 minutes over medium heat, sauté the carrots and potatoes in it.
Cook for 2 minutes after adding the lentils and turmeric.
Season with salt and pepper after adding the vegetable stock and tomato paste.
Boil the soup for about 15 minutes over low heat. Using a hand blender, puree in cream.
Dice bread slices at the same time.
In a separate pan, heat the remaining oil. Over medium heat, toast the bread cubes for 5 minutes or until golden brown.
Clean the basil leaves by shaking them dry and plucking the leaves.
Fill bowls halfway with broth, drizzle with cream, and top with bread cubes and basil.

Servings: 6

 Calories: 200

 ready in 30 min

BARLEY AND VEGETABLE SOUP

Ingredients:

3/4 cup pearl barley
4 cups vegetable stock
2 tbsp. extra-virgin olive oil
1 1/2 cup onion crumbled
1 cup carrots, chopped
1 celery stalk, chopped
1 cup mushrooms, thinly sliced
parsley (half bunch)
approx 30 mg purine

Instructions:

Add the barley with 3 cups vegetable stock in a saucepan.
Over medium heat, boil, cover for 1 hour or until the liquid is absorbed.
Meanwhile, in a large pot, heat the olive oil and add the onion, carrots, celery, and mushrooms.
Cook, covered, for 5 minutes, or until the vegetables soften.
Add remaining vegetable stock and cover and cook for 30 minutes
Cook for another 5 minutes with the barley.
Season to taste with salt and serve in bowls.
Garnish with fresh parsley chopped on top.

Servings: 8

Calories: 160

ready in 40min

CHICKEN NOODLE SOUP

Ingredients:

1 ½ cup long carrots, sliced
1 ½ cup long celery stalks
1 cup finely diced yellow onion
3 minced garlic cloves about a tbsp
2 ½ cups red potatoes, cubed into
1/2-inch cubes
6 to 7 cups of water
2 vegan bouillon cubes
1 tbsp thyme (dried)
2 cups brown spiral noodles
fresh parsley and lemon juice as an
optional for garnish
approx 22 mg purine

Instructions:

Prepare all vegetables and spices and set
them aside.
In a large pot, boil 6 cups of water, then
add the bouillon cubes, thyme, salt,
whisking to dissolve.
Add in a pot all vegetables (carrots,
celery, onion, garlic, and potatoes) and
spices. Bring to a boil, stirring
constantly. When the water boils, reduce
to low heat, cover, cook for around 10
minutes, or until the carrots and
potatoes are tender but not thoroughly
cooked. Add pasta and
return to a boil over medium-high heat
for another 10 min or until the pasta is
tender but firm. Check for salt and add a
nice grind of freshly ground black
pepper.
Before eating, garnish with freshly
chopped parsley and a squeeze of lemon
juice.

Servings: 5

Calories: 342

ready in 25min

DETOX POTATO TUMERIC SOUP

Ingredients:

4 big shallots
1 tbsp coconut oil
1/4 cup ginger, chopped
4 peeled garlic cloves, smashed with
the side of a knife
1 big peeled and diced sweet potato
2 big carrots, peeled and chopped
1 tsp of turmeric
cayenne pepper + 1/2 tsp black
pepper
4 cups vegetable stock
6 tbsp almond butter
1 coconut milk can (15 oz.)
1 Lemon juice
approx 70 mg purine

Instructions:

Add the coconut oil to a large pot
over medium-high heat. Add the
shallots and let them fry for 3-4
minutes. Add the garlic and ginger
and fry for one more minute. Add
the sweet potato, carrots, turmeric,
sea salt, black pepper, and cayenne
and stir the pot for about 30
seconds.
Add the stock to the pot and boil.
Reduce the heat to medium and
simmer for 10 minutes, or until the
vegetables are soft.
Transfer the soup to your blender,
add the almond butter, and blend
until smooth. Pour the soup back
into the pot, add the coconut milk
and lime juice, and heat through.

Servings: 6

Calories: 230

ready in 60 min

YAM AND GUNGO SOUP

Ingredients:

2 cups yams peeled and cubed
2 cups pigeon peas
70 oz water
2 cloves garlic crushed
2 stalks of spring onion
1 large green pepper
1 whole scotch bonnet of chili
3 sprigs of thyme
6 whole pimentos
approx 25 mg purine

Instructions:

Peel, then chop the yams into medium-sized chunks.
Finely chop the pimentos, garlic, and onion.
Boil the peas and yams until almost cooked for about 20 minutes.
Add all other ingredients and simmer for about 30 minutes until the broth thickens.

DESSERTS

Servings: 2

 Calories: 426

 ready in 12,15 h

OVERNIGHT OATS WITH APPLE& WALNUTS

Ingredients:

1 tsp cinnamon, salt

3 tbsp buckwheat flakes

1 cup milk (3.5 percent fat)

1 tbsp of applesauce (no added sugar)

2 tbsp chia seeds

1 apple

1 tbsp maple syrup

2 tbsp walnut kernels

approx 22 mg purine

Instructions:

Mix the buckwheat flakes with a pinch of salt and cinnamon. Stir in the milk, applesauce, and 1 tbsp chia seeds, then chill for at least 2 hours, preferably overnight.

The following day, wash, fifth, and core the apple. One half should be cut into fine wedges, while the other half should be cut into cubes. In a saucepan, combine the apple cubes and the remaining cinnamon; heat and allow to caramelize for 2-3 minutes.

Meanwhile, coarsely chop the walnuts. In two bowls or sealable glasses, place overnight oats. Arrange apple wedges, caramelized apple blocks, and walnuts on top, spread the remaining chia seeds, and cover oats with apple and walnuts.

SPICY KERNELS

Ingredients:

¼ tsp powdered cloves
¼ tsp cardamom powder
¼ tsp cinnamon
1 cup Almond kernels
1 cup Cashew nuts
3 tbsp coconut oil (liquid)
4 tbsp sugar
approx 10 mg purine

Instructions:

Spread the kernels on a baking sheet lined with baking paper and roast for around 10 minutes at 200°C / 400 F in a preheated oven.
Remove from the oven and set aside to cool for 10 minutes. Combine the spices in a bowl with the almonds, cashew nuts, coconut oil, sugar, kernels, and spice mixture. Fill a glass with a lid with 50 g of each and package it as a gift.

CHERRY YOGURT POPSICLES

Ingredients:

1 ½ cup greek yogurt
1 cup organic lime (zest and juice)
½ cup cherries (fresh)
1 tbsp powdered birch sugar
approx 12 mg purine

Instructions:

Using a hand blender, puree the cherries with powdered birch sugar as finely as possible. Strain through a fine sieve and combine yogurt, lime zest, and juice in a mixing bowl. Pour the mixture into six ice cream molds and freeze. Allow for 1 hour of freezing time, then insert wooden handles and freeze for another 3 hours. To serve, remove the ice from the molds. Fresh cherries should be washed and arranged on a tart dish as desired before decorating ice cream.

Servings: 8   Calories: 116   Ready in 10min

VEGAN AVOCADO DESSERT

Ingredients:

1 vanilla bean
1/4 cup cocoa powder (unsweetened)
1 cup freshly squeezed orange juice
1 orange with its zest
1 tbsp sugar de coco
1 tbsp cocoa nibs
approx 8 mg purine

Instructions:

Scoop avocado flesh into a blender with a spoon, then add vanilla bean seeds.

Combine the cocoa powder, orange juice, orange zest, coconut sugar, and salt in a large mixing bowl. Blend until smooth, scraping down the sides of the blender to get every last drop.

The texture should be silky and creamy. Add more orange juice or a splash of water if necessary.

Divide pudding among 8 4-6 oz. Ramekins or small bowls and chill until slightly firm, at least 2 hours. Sprinkle with cocoa nibs and cover; chill until ready to serve!

BAKED BANANA

Ingredients:

2 cups ripe bananas (four ripe bananas)
1 cup skyr
1 tbsp of linseed oil
4 tbsp almond kernels, grated
1 tbsp maple syrup
approx 20 mg purine

Instructions:

Wash the bananas without peeling them, pat them dry, and put them on an oven shelf. Bake for around 10 minutes at 200°C / 390 F in a preheated oven until the shell is evenly black.
Meanwhile, cut the vanilla pod half lengthwise and scrape the pulp out with a knife. Blend the skyr and linseed oil until smooth. For 3 minutes, roast the almonds in a hot pan without fat over medium heat. Remove the bananas from the oven. Remove the top half of the peel from
the hot fruits and set aside.
Distribute the skyr among four plates and top with the bananas. Serve with a drizzle of maple syrup and a sprinkling of almonds.

Servings: 2

Calories: 472

Ready in 20min

MILLET AND PEAR MUESLI

Ingredients:

½ cup millet
1 cup pears (2 pears)
3 tbsp walnut kernels
1 cup curd milk (1.5% fat)
1 tbsp liquid honey
1 pinch cinnamon
approx 55 mg purine

Instructions:

Put the millet in a saucepan with twice the amount of water, boil, and let it swell over low heat for about 10 minutes.
In the meantime, wash the pears, rub dry, quarter, core, and dice.
Roughly chop the walnut kernels with a large knife or a lightning chopper.
Transfer the millet to a bowl and let it cool down a bit, stirring occasionally.
Mix the curd, honey, and cinnamon.
Mix in the diced pear and millet.
Sprinkle the muesli with the walnuts and serve.

Servings: 4

Calories: 238

Ready in 20min

SKYR WITH PASSION FRUIT SAUCE

Ingredients:

2 cups skyr

1 tbsp agave syrup

6 passion fruit

1 tsp cornstarch

1 large oranges

1 tbsp honey

3 tbsp almond kernels

approx 15 mg purine

Instructions:

Mix the skyr with agave syrup and place it in the refrigerator. In the meantime, halve the passion fruit for the sauce, remove the pulp and mix with the cornstarch.

Squeeze the orange. Simmer the juice with passion fruit mixture and honey for about 3–4 minutes while stirring over low heat. Let the thickened passion fruit sauce cool for about 5 minutes.

In the meantime, roughly chop the almonds. Divide the skyr among four plates, smooth out a little, cover with the sauce and sprinkle with the almonds

Servings: 2

Calories: 416

Ready in 25min

PROTEIN PANCAKES

Ingredients:

2 tbsp almond flour

2 tbsp spelled flour

2 tbsp Quark (20 % fat)

1 tbsp baking powder (tartar)

Cinnamon, 1 pinch

1 tsp powdered vanilla

¼ cup Milk,

4 tbsp rapeseed oil

1 tbsp almonds (toasted)

2 tbsp Blueberries (60 g)

1 tbsp maple syrup (optional)

1 tbsp butter made from almonds

approx 18 mg purine

Instructions:

Whisk the eggs, almond flour, spelled flour, quark, baking powder, cinnamon, vanilla powder, and milk in a big mixing bowl. Add a splash of milk if the batter is too stiff.

In a non-stick pan, heat 2 tbsp of oil, pour 1 tbsp of batter into each pan, and bake 4–6 pancakes for 3–4 minutes on both sides over medium heat.

Toast the almond slivers for 2-3 minutes in a hot, non-stick skillet over medium heat.

Blueberries should be washed and dried before being used. Garnish the pancakes with berries, almond butter, maple syrup, and sliced almonds on top, and serve.

RED DESSERT

Ingredients:

For the Red cream;
2 ½ cups guava nectar
⅓ cup of sugar
a quarter tsp of cinnamon
⅛ tsp nutmeg
1/4 cup tapioca starch (quick-cooking)
1/2 gallon of water
1 tsp extract de Vanille

To make the Vanilla Cream;
1/2 gallon whole milk
1/2 cup lower fat cream
1 bean of vanilla
3 big yolks of eggs
1 tsp of sugar
approx 14 mg purine

Instructions:

For the Red cream: Bring guava nectar and sugar to a boil in a medium saucepan.
Add the salt, cinnamon, and nutmeg and mix well. Mix the water and fast-cooking tapioca in a small pot. Gradually pour the tapioca mixture into the saucepan, stirring constantly.
Bring to a boil once more, continuously stirring. When the tapioca grains are transparent, remove them from the heat. It should take about 13 minutes to complete this task. Add the vanilla extract and mix well. Let it cool.

To make the vanilla cream: Mix milk and cream in a medium saucepan. Scrape the seeds from the vanilla bean into the milk mixture, add the split vanilla bean to the milk. Bring the milk mixture to a low boil, then turn off the fire. Take out the vanilla bean pods.
In a medium mixing cup, whisk together the egg yolks and sugar. Whisk the hot milk mixture into the yolk mixture gradually. Return the custard to the saucepan and cook, constantly stirring, over low heat until it thickens. This will take about 5 minutes (do not boil). Pour the sauce into a pot, cover it, and keep it in the refrigerator until ready to use.
Fill the glass and combine both creams.

Servings: 3

Calories: 349

Ready in 10min

FRUIT QUARK WITH LINSEED OIL

Ingredients:

3 tbsp low-fat quark

3 tbsp milk (1.5 percent fat)

2 tbsp organic cold-pressed linseed oil

1 tbsp lemon juice

1 handful of your favorite fruit (banana, raspberries, or strawberries)

1 tbsp flax seeds, crushed (or almond slivers)

1 tsp honey (at will)

approx 12 mg purine

Instructions:

In a blender or hand blender, thoroughly combine all ingredients except the fruit.

To finish, chop the fruit into bite-size pieces and sprinkle with flax seeds or almond slivers. Combine the quark and fruit in serving bowls.

If necessary, sweeten the quark with honey.

QUARK DESSERT

Ingredients:

2 cups low fat quark
1 tbsp honey liquid
1 tsp vanilla
1 cup kiwi fruit
3 tbsp pistachios
approx 10 mg purine

Instructions:

Add the quark, yogurt, honey, and vanilla powder to a bowl and mix well. Peel and slice Kiwi fruit, and roughly chop Pistachios.

Divide half of the quark into a bowl, place the kiwi slices on top, drizzle with the remaining quark, and top with the pistachio nuts.

VEGAN SWEET CHERRY BARS

Ingredients:

1 cup rye, spelled, or whole wheat flour

1 tsp powdered baking soda

1/2 tsp bicarbonate of soda

⅓ cup olive oil

¼ cup of cold water

2 tsp vanilla extract

1 cup sugar (cane or coconut)

Non-dairy milk, 1 1/4 cup

1 lemon's juice

1 ½ cup pitted and halved sweet cherries, fresh or frozen

approx 27 mg purine

Instructions:

Preheat the oven to 350 F / 170 C. A 9 x 13 rectangular baking dish should be lightly greased and lined on the bottom with a piece of rectangular parchment paper.

In a mixing bowl, combine the flours, baking powder and soda, and salt (or the bowl of a stand mixer).

In the bowl of a stand mixer or a big mixing bowl with an electric mixer, thoroughly combine the oil, water, sugar, and vanilla extract.

Mix in the non-dairy milk and lemon juice thoroughly. In two additions, add the dry ingredients, mixing on medium speed as you go. Pour 34% of the batter into your prepared baking dish until the batter is well mixed (no lumps visible). Top with the halved frozen cherries. Drop the remaining batter on top of the cherries with a spoon. Coat cherries completely in batter, with a few peeking out from under them.

Place the baking dish in the oven. Bake for 45 minutes, or until golden brown on the edges, and put on top. Allow the cake to cool fully before serving.

Servings: 2

Calories: 445

Ready in 20 min

QUARK PANCAKES WITH FRUIT

Ingredients:

1 cup low-fat quark

3 eggs

4 tbsp spelled wholemeal flour

1 tsp vanilla extract

2 tbsp baking soda

1 tbsp of coconut oil

1 ½ cup of seasonal fruits

1 tbsp honey optional

approx 37 mg purine

Instructions:

Combine the quark and eggs in a mixing bowl, add the flour, vanilla, and baking soda, and stir until a dense dough forms.

In a non-stick pan, heat the oil, add 1 tbsp of batter to each pan, and bake 4 to 6 pancakes on both sides for 3–4 minutes over medium heat. On the side, wash the fruit, cut it into small parts, and mix it well. Serve the pancakes with honey and fruit.

POTATOES AND VEGETABLES

Servings: 4

Calories: 254

Ready in 1 hour

POTATO GOULASH

Ingredients:

1 cup celeriac
1 red pepper,
1 yellow pepper
2 cups Waxy potatoes
2 onions, red
one garlic clove
1 tbsp of rapeseed oil
1 cup low sodium vegetable broth
1 tbsp powdered noble sweet paprika
cayenne
1 bunches of parsley
4 tbsp 3.5-percent-fat yogurt
approx 18 mg purine

Instructions:

Wash the peppers, split them in half, remove the seeds, and cut them into cubes. Celeriac and potatoes should be peeled and diced, and onions and garlic should be peeled and finely chopped.

Heat the rapeseed oil for 4 minutes over medium heat, sauté the onions in a big saucepan. Fry for 3–4 minutes with the garlic, potatoes, and celery. With vegetable stock, deglaze the pan. Add the spices and cook the goulash for about 30 minutes, covered, over medium heat.

Cook for 5 minutes after adding the paprika to the potato goulash. Parsley should be washed, dried, and chopped roughly. Season the goulash with salt and pepper to taste, and serve with 1 tbsp yogurt and 1 tbsp parsley.

ROSEMARY-ROASTED POTATOES

Ingredients:

2 tbsp minced fresh rosemary
3 crushed garlic cloves
1 cup/package refrigerated red
potato wedges (such as Simply
Potatoes)
1 tbsp extra virgin olive oil
1/2 tsp powdered onion
A quarter tsp of salt
a quarter tsp of pepper
approx 22 mg purine

Instructions:

Preheat the oven to 250C / 500F.
Toss the potatoes with the
remaining ingredients in a big
mixing bowl.
Mix each potato wedge thoroughly
to coat it in oil and seasonings.
Arrange the potato wedges on a
foil-lined baking sheet.
Bake for 22 minutes, or until
golden brown and soft. Serve
immediately.

Serving: 6

Calories: 250

Ready in 1 hour

SWEET POTATO PONE

Ingredients:

1 cup white or orange fresh sweet potato peeled and grated

1 tsp ground cinnamon

1 tsp ground nutmeg

1 tsp vanilla essence

2 large eggs well beaten

2 tbsp fresh coconut grated or desiccated coconut

1 cup peeled pumpkin or squash grated

grated rind of half an orange

approx 36 mg purine

Instructions:

Grease and line an oblong tin 26cm x 18 cm x 4 cm with greaseproof paper. Preheat the oven to 190 C / 370 F.

Combine all the ingredients in a large mixing bowl, and then stir in the eggs and set them aside.

Gently pour the mixture into the prepared tin. Bake for around 50-60 minutes. The finished cake should have an almost crunchy, golden topping with a firm base.

Servings: 2

 Calories: 390

 Ready in 1,2 hour

SCALLOPED POTATOES

Ingredients:

1 tbsp butter

2 cloves garlic

1 tbsp flour

1 cup milk

1 tsp salt

½ tsp pepper

3 Yukon potatoes, peeled

2 tbsps grated parmesan cheese

fresh parsley, chopped, for garnish

approx 38 mg purine

Instructions:

Preheat the oven to 350°F (180°C).
In a small pot, melt the butter and fry the garlic until it's just starting to brown.
Add the flour, salt, and pepper. Whisk until there are no lumps. Slowly drizzle in the milk while constantly whisking to ensure a smooth mixture.
Bring to a boil, then remove from heat.
Slice the potatoes into about ⅛-inch (3 mm) thick slices, put them in a small baking dish.
Pour the sauce on top of the potatoes, then sprinkle with parmesan.
Bake for about 1 hour, until the top, is bubbly and golden brown.
Sprinkle chopped parsley on top, then serve.

KARTOFFEL-BLUMENKOHL-CURRY

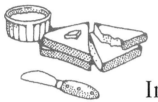

Ingredients:

2 tbsp ginger

3 cups potatoes (7 potatoes)

1 chili pepper, orange

two onions

2 tbsp ghee (clarified butter)

2 tsp turmeric powder (optional)

1 tsp cumin (black)

1 tsp coriander seeds, crushed

½ tsp mustard seed

2 cups vegetable broth

cayenne pepper

5 tomatillos

1 mango (ripe)

2 tbsp parsley

2 whole curry leaves

1 tbsp coriander

1 tsp lemon juice

Wholemeal flatbread 1 cup

1 cup plain yogurt (1.5 percent fat)

1 cup cauliflower

approx 50 mg purine

Instructions:

Trim the cauliflower, wash it, and cut it into tiny florets. The potatoes should be peeled, washed, and cut into bits. Cook the cauliflower and potatoes in boiling water until soft. Rinse and set aside. Peel ginger and dice finely. Cut the chili half lengthwise, core it, wash it, and chop it. Onions should be peeled, halved, and cut into very fine strips. In a saucepan, melt the ghee. Three minutes over medium heat, sauté the onions with chili and ginger.

Saute for 2 minutes with turmeric, black cumin, coriander, and mustard seeds. Deglaze with stock. Add the cooked vegetables, season with salt and pepper, and cook, occasionally stirring, for about 10 minutes over low heat. Clean, wash, slice, and dice the tomatoes in the meantime. Dice the mango after peeling it and removing the pulp from the block. Wash and roughly chop the parsley, curry leaves, and coriander, reserving some for garnish; stir the remaining parsley, curry leaves, and coriander into the curry, along with the tomatoes and mango, and cook for another 15 minutes. Add lemon juice, salt, and pepper. Serve the curry with flatbread and yogurt, garnished with the set-aside herbs.

Servings: 4

Calories: 688

Ready 1,15 hour

POTATO AND CHEESECAKE

Ingredients:

3 cups floury potatoes

2 tbsp fresh parsley

4 tbsp whole mountain cheese (low fat in dry matter)

2 cups mushrooms

4 shallots

3 tbsp spelled wholemeal flour

1 egg and 2 yolks of eggs

cayenne pepper

1 tsp spice nutmeg

2 tbsp breadcrumbs (whole grain)

rapeseed oil, 3 tbsp

½ cup of butter

1 tsp lemon juice

3 juniper berries, dried

approx 50 mg purine

Instructions:

Wash the potatoes and place them in a saucepan with enough water to cover them. Season with salt, bring to a boil, and boil for 25 minutes, covered, over medium heat. Meanwhile, wash the parsley, shake it dry, and chop it. Grate the cheese finely.

Clean the mushrooms and cut them in half or quarters, depending on how big they are. Shallots should be peeled, halved lengthwise, and cut into wedges.

After draining and letting the water evaporate, peel and mash the potatoes. Combine the parsley, butter, flour, and egg in a mixing bowl. Season with salt, pepper, and freshly grated nutmeg, then mix until smooth. CONTINUE TO THE NEXT PAGE

POTATO AND CHEESECAKE

Instructions:

Shape the mixture into 12–16 balls, flatten them, and roll them in breadcrumbs. In a pan, heat 12 tbsps of oil. 3–4 cakes should be fried in it for 3–4 minutes on each side over medium heat. Repeat the remaining mixture and keep the cakes warm in the oven at 80° C / 170 F.

Melt the butter in a saucepan over low heat, remove it, and set it aside to cool. Meanwhile, season the egg yolks with salt and pepper in a metal bowl with 1 tsp lemon juice.

In a saucepan, bring some water to a temperature of 80 degrees Celsius. Place the bowl containing the egg yolks on the saucepan and whisk the contents until creamy. While stirring, drizzle in the butter in a thin stream. Crush the juniper berries very finely in a mortar, then season the sauce with them. Cover and keep warm.

Brush the remaining oil on a grill pan and heat it. Grill the porcini mushrooms and shallots in it for 2-3 minutes over medium to high heat. Remove from the heat and season with salt and pepper to taste, as well as the remaining lemon juice. Serve the potato and cheese, as well as the mushroom mixture, on plates with the sauce.

Servings: 2

 Calories: 670

 Ready in 25 min

WINTER BOWL WITH POTATO

Ingredients:

1 tbsp rapeseed oil

½ tsp paprika powder

2 cups waxy potatoes

2 eggs

1 handful herbs (mixed)

1 cup fat-free quark

1 tbsp of linseed oil

cayenne

Lamb's lettuce

½ cup carrot,

1 tbsp hazelnut kernels

1 red onion, tiny

red wine vinegar, 2 tbsp

Vegetable broth, 2 tbsp

4 tbsp mustard

oil from hazelnuts

approx 58 mg purine

Instructions:

Boil the potatoes for 10 minutes. Then drain and set aside for 5 minutes to cool. After that, peel the potatoes and cut them into tiny cubes. In a pan, heat the rapeseed oil. Fry the potatoes for 5–7 minutes over medium heat, until crispy. Salt and paprika to taste, and keep warm in the pan.

Boil the eggs for 6–7 minutes in boiling water. Drain the eggs, rinse them in cold water, peel them, and break them lengthwise in half. Wash the herbs, shake them off, and cut them finely. Then combine quark, linseed oil, 3 tbsps water, salt, and pepper in a mixing bowl. The lamb's lettuce should be cleaned, washed, and dried.

Slice the carrot and wash it before cutting it into long strips. Chop the hazelnuts into small pieces. Peel the onion and finely chop it. Whisk together the vinegar, broth, butter, and mustard to make the dressing. After that, season with salt and pepper and add the onions.

Combine the potatoes, carrots, lamb's lettuce, and eggs in two cups. Drizzle dressing over the salad and hazelnuts.

COTTAGE CHEESE ON POTATO TOAST

Ingredients:

2 sweet potatoes
1 carrot
3 basil stems
1 cup Cottage cheese (10 percent fat)
cayenne
powdered paprika
2 leaves red cabbage
approx 10 mg purine

Instructions:

Peel sweet potatoes, cut each into six thin slices, and toast for around 10 minutes in a toaster or bake for 10 minutes in a 200 C / 390 F preheated oven.
Clean, wash, and coarsely grate the carrot in the meantime. Wash the basil and shake it dry before plucking a few leaves aside and chopping the rest—season with salt, pepper, paprika, cottage cheese, carrot, and chopped basil. Cut the red cabbage leaves into fine strips after washing them. Top sweet potato slices with cottage cheese and red cabbage strips, as well as basil leaves.

Servings: 4

Calories: 311

Ready 40 min

SWEET POTATO SALAD

Ingredients:

2 cups sweet potatoes (1 big sweet potato)

salt

Cheyenne pepper

1 tsp. curry powder

3 tbsp olive oil

1 cup spinach (baby)

1 lemon

2 tbsp walnut kernels

2 apples (green)

2 tbsp vegetable broth

4 tbsp quinoa puffed

1 handful chive herb

approx 36 mg purine

Instructions:

Peel and cut the sweet potato into bite-sized bits. Place on a baking sheet lined with baking paper and season with salt, pepper, one pinch of curry, and 1 tbsp of oil.

Bake the sweet potato for 20 minutes at 200°C /390 F in a preheated oven, turning it halfway through. Remove from the oven and set aside to cool for 10 minutes.

Meanwhile, clean and wash the spinach. Cut the lemon in half and squeeze the juice out. Chop the walnuts coarsely. Apples should be cleaned, washed, quartered, and cored before being cut into small pieces and drizzled with half the lemon juice.

Combine the remaining lemon juice, salt, pepper, and the remaining oil to make a dressing.

Combine the prepared ingredients with the dressing in a mixing bowl and divide them into four bowls. Sprinkle Quinoa and chive over the salad.

Servings: 4

Calories: 505

Ready 1 hour

SAUERKRAUT KUMPIR

Ingredients:

8 big waxy potatoes

2 tsp rapeseed oil

2 cups sauerkraut

1 cup plain yogurt (1.5 percent fat)

1 tsp caraway seed

salt

cayenne pepper

2 carrots

1 pear

1 tbsp of lemon juice

4 coriander stems

2 tbsp walnut kernels

One piece of 50 g gouda (45 percent fat in dry matter)

4 tbsp butter (room temperature)

approx 38 mg purine

Instructions:

Wash the potatoes, poke them several times with a fork, brush with oil, and bake for 45 minutes at 200 C / 390 F in a preheated oven until tender. Meanwhile, remove the sauerkraut and combine it with the yogurt and caraway seeds, seasoning to taste. Clean, wash, and grate the carrots and pears coarsely, then combine with the lemon juice. Wash the coriander, shake it out, and chop the leaves.

Roughly chop walnuts and roast for 3 minutes in a hot pan without fat over medium heat. Remove the potatoes from the oven, cut them lengthwise, and use a fork to loosen the insides. Combine butter and Gouda cheese in a mixing bowl. Fill the potatoes with sauerkraut, pear, carrot mixture, and roasted walnuts and coriander before serving.

FRIED POTATO & ASPARAGUS PAN

Ingredients:

2 cups green asparagus

5 shallots

3 cups small waxy potatoes

1 tbsp clarified butter

3 parsley stems

cayenne pepper

approx 18 mg purine

Instructions:

Wash potatoes and boil for 15 minutes in salted water.

Meanwhile, wash the asparagus, peel the bottom third, and trim the woody ends. Boil the asparagus for 8 minutes in salted boiling water. Drain, and break into pieces diagonally.

Drain the potatoes, let them cool down before cutting them half lengthwise.

Cut shallots into wedges after peeling them.

In a high pan, melt the clarified butter. Fry the potatoes over medium heat, frequently turning, for 10 minutes, or until golden brown.

Wash the parsley, shake it dry and chop it.

Combine the shallots and potatoes in a pan and cook for 4 minutes. Stir in the asparagus and cook for another 2 minutes, turning frequently.

Add salt, pepper, and parsley to the fried potato and asparagus pan.

SWEET POTATO&CARROT GRATIN

Ingredients:

1 cup milk
2 cups sweet potatoes
1 ½ cup carrots
½ cup creme fraiche low fat
3 eggs
half bunch fresh thyme
½ cup Gruyère cheese (1 piece)
freshly ground pepper
nutmeg, freshly grated
2 tbsp pumpkin seeds
approx 23 mg purine

Instructions:

Peel and thinly slice the sweet potatoes and carrots. In a baking dish, alternately layer the vegetable slices.
Combine the milk, crème fraîche, and eggs in a large mixing bowl. Pick the leaves off the thyme after it has been washed and dried.
To taste, combine half of the thyme and half of the cheese in a mixing bowl: salt, pepper, and nutmeg. Pour the egg milk over the vegetables and mix well. On top, sprinkle the remaining cheese and pumpkin seeds. Beak for 45 minutes at 180 C/350 F in a preheated oven. Serve with the remaining thyme as a garnish.

PEANUT&SWEET POTATO SOUP

Ingredients:

3 cups sweet potatoes

1 cup carrots

1 shallot

2 cloves garlic

1 red chili pepper

2 tbsp olive oil

1 tsp turmeric powder (optional)

1 tsp curry powder

2 cups vegetable broth, cayenne

2 cups coconut beverage

1 cup pak choi baby

4 tbsp peanut kernels, roasted

2 tbsp fresh parsley

2 tbsp Peanut butter

2 tbsp 3.5-percent-fat yogurt

1 tbsp black sesame seeds

approx 42 mg purine

Instructions:

Prepare the sweet potatoes and carrots by peeling, washing, and dicing them. Shallots and garlic should be peeled and diced finely. Cut the chili half lengthwise, core it, wash it, and chop it. In a saucepan, heat the oil. In it, sauté shallot, garlic, and chili for a few minutes.

Cook for 3 minutes on medium heat. Sauté sweet potatoes and carrots for 4 minutes, seasoning with turmeric and curry powder. Then add broth to deglaze, season with salt and pepper, and top with a coconut drink. Cook the soup for 20 minutes over low heat. Meanwhile, clean and wash the pak choy before cutting it into strips. Chop the peanuts into small pieces. Parsley should be washed, dried, and chopped. Cook for 5–8 minutes after adding the pakchoi and peanut butter to the soup. Season with salt and pepper.

Drizzle 1 tsp yogurt over the soup and garnish with the remaining peanuts, sesame seeds, and parsley on deep plates.

Servings: 4

Calories: 241

Ready 30 min

POTATO AND RADISH SALAD

Ingredients:

1 cup vegetable broth
4 cups waxy potatoes
1 mild onion
4 tbsp apple cider vinegar
1 tbsp of grainy mustard
cayenne
1 cup radish
2 handfuls of Rocket
half bunch chives
rapeseed oil, 3 tbsp
approx 24 mg purine

Instructions:

Boil the potatoes for 20–30 minutes. Then drain, let them cool, peel and slice.
Peel and finely dice the onion. Bring the broth to a boil, then add in the onion. Remove from heat and set aside for 5 minutes to steep. Season the marinade with salt and pepper after adding the vinegar and mustard.
Prepare the radishes by washing, cleaning, and slicing them. The Rocket should be washed and cleaned before being shaken dry. Break the chives into rolls after washing them. Combine the marinade with potatoes and set aside
for 30 minutes to steep.
Mix all ingredients in a salad bowl, season to taste, and serve.

AUBERGINES

Ingredients:

2 large aubergines
½ medium onion chopped
2 cloves garlic minced
2 medium tomatoes chopped
1 tsp curry powder
freshly ground black pepper
small bunch coriander finely chopped
approx 20 mg purine

Instructions:

Wash aubergines and make slits in them with a knife, then stuff the slits with the garlic and roast over a gas hob or grill until soft.

Slice in half, scrape out the pulp, and mash with all the ingredients using a fork.

Gently cook in a non-stick frying pan for 5 -7 minutes. Serve in a roti or as a side dish to curried meat or fish.

SMOOTHIE

TEA

AYURVEDIC TEA

Ingredients:

1 tsp fennel seeds
1 tsp peppercorns
6 Cardamom capsules,
2 tbsp ginger root
2 garlic cloves
3 anise stars
1 piece of cinnamon
approx 0 mg purine

Instructions:

In a mortar, grind the pepper and fennel for a few seconds. Using the back of a knife, crack open the cardamom pod. Ginger should be washed and cut into small bits.

Toast the spices in a hot saucepan over medium heat for a few minutes. Bring to a boil with the ginger and around 35oz of water. Cook for approximately 25-30 minutes on low heat.

Divide the tea you made into four cups after draining it.

ROSEMARY TEA

Ingredients:

1 rosemary branch
1 green tea bag
1 orange
approx 0 mg purine

Instructions:

Rinse the rosemary, shake it out, and put it in a mug.
Make a tea with the tea bag and 200 ml of water, as directed on the box, and top with the rosemary.
Take the orange and squeeze it.
Remove the teabag from the rosemary tea and stir in the orange juice.

Servings: 2

 Calories: 29

 Ready in 15min

CINNAMON BLOSSOM TEA

Ingredients:

1 cardamom pod
1 tsp cinnamon blossoms
1 tsp black tea or rooibos tea
8 tbsp Milk (1.5 percent fat; preferably long-life milk)
1 tsp cocoa powder (without sugar)
a liquid sweetener
approx 0 mg purine

Instructions:

In a small saucepan, bring the cinnamon blossoms, tea, cardamom, and 14oz water to a boil, then reduce to low heat and simmer for 8-10 minutes.
Meanwhile, warm the milk in a separate saucepan. Whisk in the cocoa powder and beat the mixture to a fine-pored foam with a milk frother or whisk.
Strain cinnamon blossom tea into mugs or cups and sweeten with liquid sweetener to taste. Place the cocoa foam on top of the cake.

Servings: 1

Calories: 2

Ready in 15 min

NETTLE AND BIRCH LEAF TEA

Ingredients:

2 tsp dried birch leaf
4 tsp dried nettle leaves
2 tsp dried juniper berry
1 lemon (organic)
approx 0 mg purine

Instructions:

Lightly mash the juniper berries in a mortar or with a big knife.

Combine nettle and birch leaves in a saucepan and add 1 cup of boiling water. Allow for an 8-minute rest period after covering.

While you're waiting, wash the lemon in hot water and pat it dry with a paper towel. Thinly peel the peel and cut it into fine strips with a peeler.

Strain the tea into a mug or glass using a sieve. Serve with lemon zest strips as a garnish.

GOUT AND JOINT PAIN JUICE

Ingredients:

half of a lemon
1-inch piece peeled ginger root
approx 0 mg purine

Instructions:

Run the ingredients through the juicer one by one. Drink the juice once a day.

Servings: 2

Calories: 245

Ready in 5min

ANTI-INFLAMMATORY SMOOTHIE

Ingredients:

1 cup Frozen Strawberries
½ can Coconut Milk
1 tsp ginger (fresh)
Cherry Juice (1-2 oz.)natural
approx 10 mg purine

Instructions:

In a blender, add all ingredients and puree until smooth.

Servings: 2

Calories: 185

Ready in 10 min

VANILLA BLACK TEA SMOOTHIE

Ingredients:

1 cup black tea
½ cup almond milk
1 tbsp vanilla protein powder
½ cup plain yogurt
1 banana, sliced
1 cup blueberry
2 cups ice
sliced almond, for serving
approx 14 mg purine

Instructions:

Add the black tea, almond milk, protein powder, yogurt, banana, blueberries, and ice to a blender. Blend until smooth.
Serve in a glass-topped with sliced almonds.

Servings: 4

Calories: 153

Ready in 15min

PERSIMMON LASSI

Ingredients:

3 persimmons
1 organic lime
2 cups plain yogurt (1.5 % fat)
2 tsp powdered cardamom
1 tsp honey
6 ice cubes
approx 8 mg purine

Instructions:

Clean, wash, and cut the persimmons into quarters. The lime should be washed, dried, and the peel removed.
In a blender, combine the persimmon, honey, lime zest, yogurt, cardamom, and ice cubes and blend on high until a smooth consistency. If possible, add a splash of cold water or lime juice. Serve cold, divided among four glasses.

Servings: 2

Calories: 495

Ready in 5 min

COFFEE SMOOTHIE

Ingredients:

2 frozen bananas
Coconut water 1 cup
cocoa powder 2 tbsp
4 tbsp espresso coffee
approx 11 mg purine

Instructions:

Combine all ingredients in a blender and puree until smooth. Pour into two glasses and serve chilled.

CHERRY "CHEESECAKE" SMOOTHIE

Ingredients:

1 ¼ cup unsweetened coconut milk
¾ cup cherries, frozen
1 tbsp of coconut oil
1 tsp lemon juice (optional)
2 tsp extract de vanille
1 tsp raw honey or pure maple syrup
1 tbsp protein powder (unflavored)
approx 8 mg purine

Instructions:

In a high-powered blender, mix
the cashews and coconut milk until
smooth (1-2 minutes).
Mix for another minute on high
with the remaining ingredients.
Add ¼ cup more water or coconut
milk if the smoothie is too thick
for you.

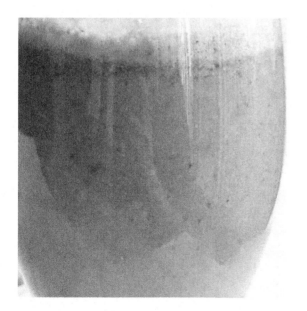

Servings: 25

Calories: 33

Ready in 15 min

HEALTHY GREEN SHOT

Ingredients:

2 pears
3 green apples (e.g., granny smith)
3 stalk Celery
4 tbsp Ginger (organic)
1 bunch parsley
3 kilograms of kiwifruit
2 Lime
Turmeric, 1 tsp
approx 18 mg purine

Instructions:

Peel, wash, and cut pears, apples, celery, ginger, and parsley. Using a spoon, scrape the pulp from the kiwi fruit halves. Limes should be halved, and the juice squeezed out.

In a blender mix pears, apples, kiwis, celery, ginger, and parsley.

Season with turmeric and freshly squeezed lime juice. Serve the mixture as shots right away or portion it out and freeze it.

Servings: 3

Calories: 80

Ready in 5min

CHERRY CHOCOLATE SMOOTHIE

Ingredients:

8 ounces coconut water
2 cups fresh or frozen pitted cherries
1 ice cube
2 tbsp cocoa powder (unsweetened)
optional garnish: chopped cherries
approx 9 mg purine

Instructions:

Place cherries, coconut water, ice, and unsweetened cocoa powder in a blender and blend until smooth. As an optional garnish, top with sliced fresh cherries.

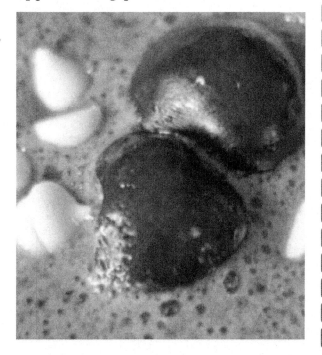

Servings: 2

Calories: 218

Ready in 10min

MANGO AND BANANA SMOOTHIE

Ingredients:

1 small ripe mango
5 oranges
1 banana,
1 cup Yogurt (low-fat)
approx 18 mg purine

Instructions:

Squeeze the oranges to get the juice.
Blend a banana, mango after
removing the skin, yogurt, and
orange juice until smooth.
Serve in two glasses.

PASTA

RICE

ZUCCHINI SPAGHETTI

Ingredients:

1 (7-ounce) can of chipotle chiles in adobo sauce

1 hot chili

2 cups spaghetti

2 tbsp olive oil

2 minced garlic cloves

4 cups shredded zucchini

a quarter tsp of salt

a quarter tsp of black pepper

2 tbsp grated Parmesan cheese

approx 32 mg purine

Instructions:

Cook pasta as directed on the box. Remove the seeds from the chili (leave the seeds in for extra heat); mince the chile. In a wide nonstick skillet, heat the oil over medium-high heat. Sauté for 1 minute with the chili, sauce, and garlic.

Add the zucchini and cook for 4 minutes, stirring continuously.

Combine pasta and zucchini mixture in a large mixing bowl—season with salt, pepper, and parmesan cheese.

Servings: 4

Calories: 531

Ready in 30 min

LENTIL NOODLES WITH PESTO

Ingredients:

2 cups brussels sprouts
1 cup lentil noodles
1 garlic clove
5 tbsp oil-dried tomato (drained)
parmesan cheese in a single piece
2 tbsp Pinenuts
8 tbsp olive oil
2 lemons (organic) (zest and juice)
cayenne pepper
1 handful basil leaves
approx 48 mg purine

Instructions:

Thoroughly clean, wash, and cut the Brussels sprouts in half. Boil the sprouts for 5 minutes in salted water. Drain and rinse.
Meanwhile, boil the pasta as directed on the package.
Cut the dried tomatoes into small pieces in the meantime. Parmesan cheese should be grated and roast pinenuts in a hot pan without fat over medium heat.
Using a blender, finely puree the tomatoes, parmesan, pinenuts, oil, and 3–4 tbsps water. Season to taste with salt, pepper, lemon zest, and juice. Clean the basil by squeezing it dry. Serve with pesto and basil on top of the pasta and Brussels sprouts.

Servings: 1

Calories: 590

Ready in 20 min

GOAT CHEESE PASTA

Ingredients:

1 small garlic clove

2 dry tomatoes in oil

3 basil stems

60 g goat cheese

80 g pasta (whole wheat) (e.g., linguine)

cumin

approx 30 mg purine

Instructions:

Place the tomatoes in a colander and pour the oil into a small cup.
Cut the tomatoes into strips or roughly slice them with a sharp knife.
Peel and finely cut the garlic cloves.
Wash the basil leaves, shake them out, and cut them coarsely. Through your fingers, break up the goat cheese.
Cook the noodles until they are firm to the bite in plenty of salted water according to the package directions. Meanwhile, heat tomato oil in a pan over low heat fry garlic and tomatoes for a few minutes in the oil. Combine the basil and goat cheese in a bowl and stir to combine. Drain the pasta, mix in the goat cheese pasta, add fry tomatoes and garlic, and season with black pepper.

KONJAC PASTA WITH BERRIES

Ingredients:

1 lime

2 shallots

1 garlic clove

1 chili pepper (red)

3 sticks celery

rapeseed oil, 2 tbsp

Vegetable broth ½ cup

1 cup soy cream or almond cuisine

2 tbsp Pine nuts

5 big strawberries

half bunch parsley

cayenne pepper

2 cups konjac noodles

approx 28 mg purine

Instructions:

Wash the lime in hot water, pat dry, and grate some peel finely. Squeeze the juice from Lime.

Peel shallots and garlic and finely dice them. Cut the chili half lengthwise, core it, wash it, and chop it. Celery should be cleaned, threads removed if possible, washed, and cut into thick slices. Chop the celery greens coarsely.

In a pan, heat the oil. Sauté for 3–4 minutes over medium heat with shallots, garlic, chili, and celery. Use broth to deglaze the pan. Pour in the almond or soy cream, bring to a boil, and cook for 5–6 minutes, stirring occasionally.

Meanwhile, toast the pine nuts for 3 minutes in a hot pan without fat over medium heat. Strawberries should be cleaned and washed before being cut into small cubes. Parsley should be washed, dried, and chopped.

Add the parsley into the sauce and mix well—season with salt, pepper, lime zest, and juice to taste. Boil konjak spaghetti for 2 minutes in salted boiling water. Drain and combine with the herb and lime sauce. Serve on a plate of pine nuts and strawberries on top.

Servings: 2

Calories: 542

Ready in 25 min

SPAGHETTI WITH PAK CHOI

Ingredients:

1 cup whole wheat spaghetti
2 tbsp ginger
1 clove of garlic
2 pieces spring onions
2 cups pak choi
1 handful parsley
1 tbsp coconut oil
1 tbsp lime juice
pepper
chili flakes
1 tsp sesame
approx 28 mg purine

Instructions:

Boil the spaghetti in salted boiling water for about 8-10 minutes until al dente. Then drain.

In the meantime, peel and chop the ginger and garlic. Clean and wash the spring onions and cut them into rings. Clean and wash the pak choi and cut it into strips. Wash the parsley and shake dry.

Heat the oil in a pan, sauté the ginger, garlic, and spring onions over medium heat for 4 minutes. Add pak choi and sauté for 5 minutes, deglaze with lime juice—season with salt, pepper, and chili flakes.

Arrange the noodles on plates, pour the pak choi on top and serve sprinkled with parsley, sesame seeds, and chili flakes

Servings: 2

Calories: 266

Ready in 35 min

ZUCCHINI PASTA

Ingredients:

2 tbsp pine nuts

2 radicchio

2 cups zucchini

1 clove of garlic

1 tbsp olive oil

1 organic lemon

1 tbsp walnut oil

pepper

approx 18 mg purine

Instructions:

Roast the pine nuts in a large pan until they are fragrant. Take out and let cool. Wash the radicchio and cut it into strips.

Wash and clean the zucchini. Use a spiral cutter to cut into fine linguine strips. Peel garlic and chop finely. Wash the lemon with hot water and pat dry. Finely grate the peel and squeeze out the juice.

Heat the pine nut pan again and add the olive oil. Add the garlic, radicchio, and sauté for 1–2 minutes over low heat.

Then remove from heat and add zucchini, lemon juice, lemon zest, and walnut oil. Season with salt and pepper and season to taste. Divide between 2 plates and sprinkle with pine nuts.

Servings: 2

Calories: 629

Ready in 30min

GOAT CHEESE RICE PAN

Ingredients:

1 cup parboiled rice

1 tsp salt

2 tbsp turmeric powder

1 shallot

1 garlic clove

2 carrots

1 pepper, red

1 lime, organic

2 tbsps olive oil

cayenne pepper

4 thaler of goat cheese

1 ice cube

2 tbsp spelled wholemeal flour

3 tbsp almond flour

a quarter-bunch of basil

oil for fry

approx 20 mg purine

Instructions:

Boil rice for 16-18 minutes over low heat in 1 cup boiling salted water with turmeric. Then remove it from the heat and set it aside to steep.

Peel and cut the shallot and garlic in the meantime. Carrots and peppers should be cleaned and washed before being cut into strips. Rinse the lime in hot water, dry it, rub the peel, and squeeze the juice into a glass. In a pan, heat 1 tbsp of oil, and over medium heat, sauté the shallot and garlic for 2 minutes. Sauté for 5–7 minutes with the carrot and bell pepper strips. Cook for 2 minutes after adding the rice. Season with salt, pepper, deglazing the rice pan with lime juice and 3 tbsps of water. While the vegetables are cooking, crack an egg into a plate for the goat cheese, place flour on another plate with salt and pepper and almonds on a third plate. Toss the goat cheese thaler in flour first, then the egg, and finally into the almonds.

In a separate pan, heat the oil. Fry the goat's cheese thalers for 7–8 minutes on both sides over medium heat, until golden. Basil should be washed, dried, and chopped. Serve the goat cheese thaler alongside the rice pan and a sprig of basil on top.

Servings: 2

Calories: 250

Ready in 25 min

COUSCOUS BASE RECIPE

Ingredients:

1 cup cuscus,
1 cup water,
salt,
olive oil
approx 0 mg purine

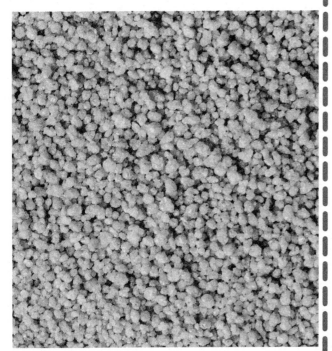

Instructions:

Fry cuscus in a pan with olive oil stir all the time with a wooden spoon until it changes the color; put the cuscus in a bowl through over salted boiling water and cover. You can boil in the water Rosmarin or thyme or some aromatic leaves if you want to. Wait for around 15 min so the couscous will absorb all water and double the volume.

COUSCOUS WITH VEGETABLES

Ingredients:

1 cup cuscus

1 cups water

2 onions,

3 carrots,

2 courgettes

2 garlic cloves,

rosemary,

olive oil,

salt

approx 12 mg purine

Instructions:

Wash and cut long way carrots and courgettes. Cut the onion and fry them in a pan with oil until soft, add carrots, and after 5 min, add courgettes.

In the end, add finely cut garlic, rosemary, and salt, cover the pan and let on medium heat for 15 minutes.

Make ready cuscus as in the base recipe. Stir cuscus with vegetables and serve.

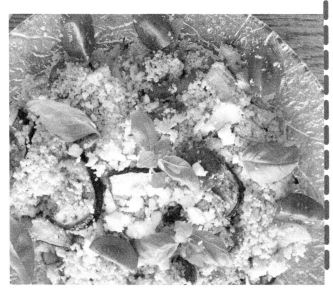

Servings: 4

Calories: 250

Ready in 20 min

COUSCOUS WITH ROSEMARY

Ingredients:

1 cup cuscus
1 cups water
2 tablespoons of soy sauce (if you wish to)
rosemary
olive oil
salt
approx 0 mg purine

Instructions:

Toasty cuscus with oil and rosemary, as described in the base recipe.
Boil water with soy sauce. Put the cuscus in the bowl through boil water on and cover. Leave for 15 min. Serve on a plate, ideally with vegetables.

Servings: 8

Calories: 160

Ready in 35 min

EASY RICE

Ingredients:

1 cup kidney beans / red peas

2 sprigs of fresh thyme

1 bay leaf

1 spring onion

1 tsp cumin powder

1 clove garlic finely chopped

½ tsp all-purpose seasoning

1 red pepper deseeded and diced

½ cup frozen mixed vegetables

1 cup basmati rice uncooked

4 tbsp coconut cream

2 cups water

approx 86 mg purine

Instructions:

Put the beans in a large pan with a tight-fitting lid and add the water. Then add all the other ingredients, except the rice, and bring to a boil. Rinse the rice in warm water before adding it to the pot. Stir well.

Cover the pan and simmer for a further 20-30 minutes or until all the liquid has been absorbed and the rice is cooked. You may need to add more liquid to soften the rice.

Servings: 4

Calories: 340

Ready in 25 min

PASTA WITH EGGS

Ingredients:

2 cups pasta
6 small courgettes,
1 onion,
half red pepper
1 leaf carbage,
2 eggs,
nutmeg,
Parmigiano Reggiano cheese,
olive oil, salt
approx 20 mg purine

Instructions:

Wash and cut on small pieces the vegetable, fry them in the oil, start with onion, pepper, cabbage leaf, and courgette; after adding salt, cover and let them fry on medium heat for 15 min.

In the meantime, boil pasta in a big pot with salted water. In one bowl, whisk eggs with nutmeg. After the pasta is boiled, drain and mix the pasta in the pan with vegetables, add a few spoons of olive oil and eggs and let them mix well for 2 minutes on medium heat. Serve with parmigiano reggiano grated chees on top.

CHICKEN

Servings: 4

Calories: 357

Ready in 20min

CHICKEN AND VEGETABLE FRIED RICE

Ingredients:

1 cup diced chicken breast

1 medium onion, diced

1 medium diced zucchini

Cut 1 ear of corn kernels

1 cup peas (green)

½ cup shelled and cooked edamame

2 cups cooked broccoli, cut into small florets

1 egg

2 cups brown rice leftovers, ideally cold

1 tbsp sesame oil

2 tbsp low-sodium soy sauce

1 tbsp of vinegar

1 cup minced scallions

approx 150 mg purine

Instructions:

Spray a wok or wide pan with non-stick spray and heat over medium-high heat. Cook chicken breasts for 4 minutes on each side. There's no need to keep moving the chicken around; let it brown and flavor.

When the chicken is finished, remove it from the pan and set it aside.

Cook for 3-4 minutes in the same pan the onion and zucchini.

Combine corn kernels, peas, edamame, and broccoli in a frying pan, and fry for 2 minutes

Arrange the vegetables around the pan's edge, then crack the egg in the middle. Scramble the egg with a wooden spoon as soon as possible.

Combine the cold brown rice, cooked chicken, and sesame oil. Stir well to disperse the oil and evenly distribute the rice and vegetables in the pan.

Allow the ingredients to brown slightly for 3 min. approx. Mix in the scallions, soy sauce, and rice vinegar.

Servings: 4

Calories: 291

Ready in 30 min

CHICKEN SALAD

Ingredients:

2 boneless, skinless chicken breasts, cooked and cut into cubes

2 celery stalks, chopped

1 tbsp red onion, chopped

1/2 cup quartered red seedless grapes

1/2 cup non-fat Greek yogurt

1 tsp powdered garlic

1 tsp freshly ground black pepper

2 halved whole-wheat pita pockets

4 lettuce leaves

approx 70 mg purine

Instructions:

Add all of the salad ingredients together in a big mixing bowl. Mix well. You can eat the chicken salad on its own or in a pita sandwich.

Servings: 8

Calories: 180

Ready 1hour

BROWN STEW CHICKEN

Ingredients:

6 chicken quarters - skin removed
1 carrot peeled and diced
1 green or red pepper finely sliced
1 cup water

Marinade
1 tsp coarsely ground black pepper
3 sprigs thyme
1 tbsp low sodium soy sauce
1 clove of garlic crushed
1 large tomato chopped
1 medium onion chopped
juice of 1 lime
scotch bonnet pepper to taste
approx 180 mg purine

Instructions:

Coat the chicken with garlic, soy sauce, onion, black pepper, lime juice, and scotch bonnet pepper. Marinate in the fridge for about 2 hours or overnight, if possible.
Preheat the oven to 190 C / 370 F. Meanwhile, mix all the other ingredients and water in the chicken marinade.
Cover with foil or a tight-fitting lid and bake in the oven for 30-40 minutes, turning frequently.

Servings: 4

Calories: 220

Ready in 20 min

CHICKEN VEGGIE

Ingredients:

2 tbsp low-sodium soy sauce, divided
1 lime juice, split
2 tbsp sesame oil (divided)
2 cups chicken breast, skinless and boneless, cut into bite-size parts
1 tbsp canola oil, expeller pressed
2 carrots, peeled and sliced into tiny rounds (about 1 cup)
2 cups broccoli florets, cut into bite-size pieces (from 1 small bunch)
1 medium zucchini, sliced lengthwise in half and then into 14-inch-thick half-moons (about 2 cups)
4 minced garlic cloves
2 green onions (white and green parts)
1 seeded and minced jalapeno pepper
¼ cup new basil, sliced
¼ cup fresh cilantro, chopped
Brown rice, if desired
approx 180 mg purine

Instructions:

In a big zip-top plastic bag or cup, combine 1 tbsp soy sauce, ginger, half a lime juice, and 1 tsp sesame oil. Place the chicken pieces in the zip-top plastic bag or cup, mix them all well, and place them in the refrigerator for 1 hour or up to 24 hours.

Heat the oil in a large wok or non-stick skillet over medium-high heat when you're ready to make your stir fry.

Stir in the chicken and the marinade for 1 minute. Stir in the carrots, broccoli, zucchini, garlic, green onions, and jalapeno pepper for a few minutes more, or until the chicken is cooked through and the vegetables are crisp-tender.

Combine the remaining 1 tbsp soy sauce, the remaining lime juice, and the remaining sesame oil in a large mixing bowl. Stir in the basil and cilantro just before serving.

If needed, serve with brown rice.

Servings: 2

Calories: 249

Ready in 45 min

CHICKEN-BROCCOLI STIR FRY

Ingredients:

1 cup low-sodium vegetable broth

1 tbsp low sodium soy sauce

1/2 tsp sesame seed, roasted

White pepper, 1/4 tsp

1/4 to 1/3 tsp thickening

2 cups boneless and skinless chicken thighs or breasts

2 cups blanched broccoli

1/3 cup sliced bell pepper

1/3 cup sliced onion

1 tbsp. minced garlic

1 tbsp. minced ginger

1 tsp of peanut oil

approx 200 mg purine

Instructions:

Prepare the broccoli by blanching it: Fill a large pot halfway with water and bring to a boil.

Separate the florets from the broccoli stem and cut the florets into smile pieces.

Keep a big bowl of ice water near the boiling water tank.

Cook the florets for two to three minutes in boiling water.

Remove the broccoli from the boiling water with a slotted spoon and put it in the ice water.

When cooled, pour into a colander to drain.

Prepare the sauce.

To a cup of vegetable broth, add 1 tsp soy sauce, sesame oil, white pepper, and Thick-It-Up.

Be sure to give it a nice stir.

Keep the sauce apart.

continue to the next page

46

Servings: 2

Calories: 249

Ready in 45min

CHICKEN-BROCCOLI STIR FRY

Instructions:

continue from the previous page

In a medium-high-heat pan, combine 1 tbsp peanut oil, 1 tbsp garlic, and 1 tbsp ginger.

Add the onion and bell pepper when the ginger and garlic are fragrant. After a few minutes of stirring, transfer all to the side in the pan.

Place the chicken in the pan's center and spread it out evenly. Allow the chicken to sit for about a minute to develop color on the exterior before flipping it over to build color on the other side. Begin stirring until the exterior of the chicken no longer appears raw.

Turn the heat up to high and stir in the stir fry sauce. Boil, then reduce to low heat and simmer for three minutes, uncovered. Stir in the broccoli and cook until tender.

Servings: 4

Calories: 349

Ready in 25min

CHICKEN WRAP

Ingredients:

2 chicken breast fillets

3 tbsp low sodium soy sauce

2 cucumbers

2 carrots

4 coriander stems

8 iceberg lettuce sheets

½ cup of peanut butter

6 tbsps coconut milk

1 tbsp extra virgin olive oil

pepper cayenne

4 tortilla cake (whole grain)

4 tbsp sour cream

approx 75 mg purine

Instructions:

Clean the chicken breasts, dry them, and cut them into strips. In a dish, add 1 tbsp soy sauce, season with salt and pepper, and marinate the chicken breast for about 10 minutes. Meanwhile, wash and cut the cucumber and carrot into fine sticks. Coriander leaves should be cleaned, shaken dry, and loosely chopped. Iceberg lettuce should be washed, dried, and cut into thin strips. Heat the peanut butter and coconut milk together in a saucepan to make the peanut coconut sauce. Season with cayenne pepper and the remaining soy sauce to taste. In a non-stick pan, heat the oil, remove the chicken breast from the marinade, and fry until golden brown on all sides over medium heat. Remove the chicken from the pan and set it aside.

In a non-stick pan, roast wraps for about 30 seconds on each hand. Then, brush one-half of each wrap with 1 tbsp sour cream and top with chicken, cucumber, carrot, and lettuce. Sprinkle coriander and drizzle with peanut and coconut sauce. From the bottom, fold in the chicken wrap and roll it up.

Servings: 4

Calories: 350

Ready in 4,30 hous

CHICKEN - GARLIC AND SESAME

Ingredients:

12 pieces chicken thighs, drumsticks, and legs
4 tbsp water or chicken broth or
1/4 cup tamari coconut aminos may be used as a substitute.
3 garlic cloves, pressed
1 tsp smoked chili pepper (smoked paprika may be substituted)
2 tsp oregano (dried)
2 tbsp apple cider vinegar (unfiltered)
Worcestershire sauce, 2 tsp
1 tbsp sesame oil (toasted)
approx 110 mg purine

Instructions:

Combine all ingredients in a cup, then pour into the slow cooker's bottom.
Arrange the chicken on top and pour in the sauce.
Cook for 4 hours on medium.
Serve with your favorite vegetables or rice or quinoa.

Servings: 4

Calories: 242

Ready in 45 min

CHICKEN STROGANOFF

Ingredients:

1 ½ cup wide egg noodles
3 tbsp. unsalted butter
1 small chopped onion
2 cups sliced white or cremini mushrooms
2 cups chicken thighs, skinless and boneless, cut into chunks
2 tbsp flour (all-purpose)
1 tsp paprika, plus additional for sprinkling
peppercorns, freshly ground
1 cup low-sodium broth
1 tbsp Worcestershire
1/2 cup sour cream plus extra to use as a topping
2 tbsp. fresh parsley, chopped
1 tsp salt
¼ tsp pepper
approx 85 mg purine

Instructions:

Boil a large pot of salted water, boil the noodles according to the package directions, and drain.

Meanwhile, in a big skillet over medium-high heat, melt 2 tbsp butter, add onion and fry for 2 minutes, or until the onion is slightly soft. Add mushrooms and fry for another 2 minutes.

Mix the chicken, paprika, salt, and pepper with the remaining 1 tbsp butter. Fry, constantly stirring, for 3 minutes, or until the chicken is golden brown.

Add the chicken broth and Worcestershire sauce. Bring to a low boil, reduce to low heat and cook until the sauce has thickened, around 5 minutes. Season with salt and pepper and stir in the sour cream. Boil gently for another 2 minutes, or until the chicken is cooked through.

Distribute the noodles between the bowls.

Add the chicken mixture, parsley, sour cream, and paprika to the top.

LEMON AND ASPARAGUS CHICKEN

Ingredients:

1 lemon, organic

2 chicken breast fillets

cayenne pepper

powdered paprika

2 tbsp whole wheat flour

2 tbsp olive oil

2 cups asparagus (green)

2 cloves garlic

1 tbsp mustard

½ cup vegetable broth low sodium

a quarter-bunch of fresh herbs (e.g., parsley or chervil)

approx 180 mg purine

Instructions:

Cut the lemon in half after washing it in hot water. Half of the juice should be squeezed and rubbed onto the peel, and half of the remaining half should be cut into slices. Cut the chicken breast fillets in half horizontally after rinsing them under cold water and patting them dry. Turn in the flour and season with salt, pepper, and paprika powder. In a pan, heat 1 tbsp of olive oil. Cook the meat for 4–5 minutes on each side over medium heat. In the meantime, toss in the lemon wedges. Take the chicken and lemon out of the pan and set them aside.

Meanwhile, wash the asparagus, pat it dry, and trim the woody ends off. Cut the asparagus into 4–5 cm long sections. Garlic should be peeled and chopped finely.

In the same pan, heat the remaining oil and fry the garlic and asparagus bits.

Stir in the lemon juice, lemon zest, mustard, and stock, then bring to a boil for a few minutes. Reduce the heat to low and return the chicken breast fillet and lemon wedges to the pan to steep for a few minutes. Season with salt and pepper to taste. Rinse the herbs, shake them off, and chop them coarsely. Sprinkle the lemon and asparagus chicken with a bit of salt and pepper.

Servings: 4

Calories: 292

Ready in 1,45 hour

CHICKEN CASSEROLE

Ingredients:

6 fresh sage leaves
1 chicken (6 pounds)
3 tbsp olive oil (distributed)
1 ½ cup peeled and trimmed carrots,
1 cup peeled and cut turnips
2 cups peeled and halved fingerling
potatoes
2 tbsp. fresh thyme, chopped
approx 175 mg purine

Instructions:

Preheat the oven to 190 C / 425 F.
Under the skin of the chicken, put
six lemon slices and sage leaves. Fill
the cavity with the rest of the lemon.
Tuck the wings under and tie the
legs together with twine.
Coat the chicken with 1 tsp of oil.
Place the chicken in a roasting pan
and roast for 1 hour 15 minutes, or
until an instant-read thermometer
reads 165°F. Allow 15 minutes for
the chicken to rest on a cutting
board.
Meanwhile, make matchsticks out
of root vegetables. Toss the
remaining oil and thyme with
potatoes in a baking tray. Cook for
45 minutes, or until soft, stirring
occasionally. Take the chicken skin
off. Take the lemons out of the
cavity and throw them away. Serve
with the vegetables.

Servings: 3

Calories: 875

Ready in 1 hour
20 min

CHEESY CHICKEN BROCCOLI BAKE

Ingredients:

1 big chicken breast
1 cup long-grain rice
¼ tsp black pepper
½ tsp onion powder
1 tbsp of cream
½ cup shredded cheddar cheese
2 cups broccoli, diced
1 ½ cups chicken broth
more cheddar cheese, for topping
approx 280 mg purine

Instructions:

Heat oven to 375°F (190°C).
In a casserole dish, combine rice, pepper, onion powder, cream, cheese, broccoli, and chicken broth.
Mix until everything is combined.
Lay chicken on top of the rice mixture. Space evenly.
Cover with foil and bake for 50 minutes.
Take off the cover and top the chicken with more cheese. Bake uncovered for another 5 minutes or until the cheese is melted.

Servings: 2

Calories: 536

Ready in 1 hour

ONE-PAN CHICKEN AND VEGGIES

Ingredients:

2 boneless, skinless chicken breasts
1 large sweet potato, diced
1 head broccoli, or a large bag of broccoli florets
4 cloves garlic, minced
2 tbsp fresh rosemary
1 tbsp paprika
salt, pepper
2 tbsps olive oil
approx 240 mg purine

Instructions:

Line a baking sheet with aluminum foil. Layout the sweet potato, chicken breasts, and broccoli.

Evenly distribute the garlic, rosemary, paprika, salt, and pepper over the entire pan. Drizzle with olive oil.

Bake at 400°F (200°C) for 35-40 minutes (or until the internal temperature of the chicken reaches 165°F (75°C), and the juices run clear).

CHICKEN WITH POTATOES

Ingredients:

1 ½ cup potatoes
1 cup tomatoes
1 bunch parsley
1 small onion
1 ½ cup breast fillet
cumin
4 tbsp of extra virgin olive oil
1 cup vegetable broth
approx 200 mg purine

Instructions:

Boil the potatoes for 15-20 minutes, then drain. Meanwhile, wash the tomatoes, cut them in half, and strain out the seeds with your hands. Wash, dry, and chop the parsley. Onions should be peeled and chopped finely. Rinse the chicken breast fillet, pat dry, and slice thinly on an angle.

Place slices between two layers of cling film, flatten with a heavy pan or a meat tenderizer to form small schnitzels.

Heat a pan over high heat and fry the tomato halves without fat on the cut surface. Take tomatoes from the pan and put them aside. In the same pan, add 2 tbsps of oil, add the chicken and cook for 2-3 minutes on each side over medium. Remove chicken from the pan and keep them aside.

In the same pan, fry for 1-minute onion, then add tomatoes and chicken schnitzel.

Cook for another 2-3 minutes, then pour the broth over them. Season with salt, pepper, and parsley. Let boil on low heat for another 5 min.

Peel and dice the potatoes. In a second pan, heat the remaining oil and fry the potatoes for about 5 minutes on all sides over medium heat. Serve potatoes with chicken.

Servings: 2

Calories: 403

Ready in 1 hour

CHICKEN VEGETABLE SOUP

Ingredients:

2 chicken breasts

1 onion

1 soup vegetable bunch (plus other aromatic vegetables such as celery or onion)

2 lemons, tiny

1 tbsp olive oil

2 tsp. black pepper

1 leaf of bay

2 leaves of lime

2 garlic cloves

2 allspice berries

1 head of kohlrabi

3 waxy potatoes

½ cup peas

2 cups water

approx 225 mg purine

Instructions:

Clean the chicken breasts by rinsing them and patting them dry with paper towels.

Peel the carrots and parsley root from the soup vegetables. Trim the celery and leeks. One carrot, half a parsley root, half a celery stalk, and the leek greens, chopped. Pluck a few celery leaves, rinse them, and set them aside. Sear the onion halves in a pot coated with oil over high heat, then remove from the pan. Fry the chicken breasts in the same oil-coated pot over medium heat.

Combine the onion halves, chopped soup vegetables, and celery leaves in a large pot. Pour in about 2 cups of water and quickly bring to a boil. Add salt, peppercorns, bay leaf, lime leaves, cloves, allspice berries, and lemon slices. With the lid ajar, cook for about 20 minutes. Continue on the next page.

Servings: 2

Calories: 403

Ready in 1 hour

CHICKEN VEGETABLE SOUP

Instructions:

Continue from the previous page...

In the meantime, roughly chop the remaining soup vegetables. Potatoes and kohlrabi should be scrubbed and peeled before being cut into uniform sections.

Remove the chicken from the pot and place it on a plate.

Strain the cooking liquid into a separate pot using a fine sieve. To taste, season with salt and pepper.

Carry potatoes and remaining soup vegetables to a simmer over medium heat. The cooking time is about 15 minutes.

Cook for another 5 minutes after adding the peas and chicken.

Move the vegetables from the pot to plates with a slotted spoon. Pour a small amount of broth onto each plate. Place the chicken on top of the vegetable broth. Serve with the remaining chopped celery leaves.

Servings: 2

Calories: 360

Ready in 1 hour

CHICKEN AND LENTIL STEW

Ingredients:

1 cup dry lentils

2 cups chicken breast

1 tsp celery seed

1 tsp coriander

1 tbsp paprika

1 tbsp seasoning (Italian)

1 cup plain greek yogurt
(reserve a few tbsp to dollop on
top at the end)

1/2 tiny orange, freshly squeezed

1 tbsp olive or coconut oil

1 chopped red onion

1/2 gallon coconut milk

1-quart chicken broth

a pinch of black pepper

garnish with parsley or cilantro

approx 350 mg purine

Instructions:

Boil 3 cups of water, add 1 cup dried green lentils and cook for 2 min. Turn heat off and let the lentils soak for 1 hour in the water. To make the chicken marinade, combine the chicken cubes with celery seed, 1/2 tsp coriander, paprika, and Italian seasoning in a mixing bowl add the greek yogurt, reserving a few tbsps to dollop on top at the end. Squeeze half an orange juice into the mixture and mix to incorporate both ingredients. Refrigerate for at least 10 minutes, up to 2 hours, with a lid or plastic wrap on top.

In the large cast iron dutch oven add 1 tbsp olive oil and marinated chicken and fry for 5 min, stirring occasionally. Toss in your chopped red onion, turn the chicken, and cook for another 5 minutes. Drain the lentils and add to the chicken, coconut milk, chicken broth, and salt/pepper. Stir to thoroughly mix, then cover and cook for 35 minutes, stirring occasionally.

Use a slotted spoon. Scoop the lentils and chicken into a bowl. Enjoy with a sprinkle of parsley and a dollop of plain Greek yogurt on top!

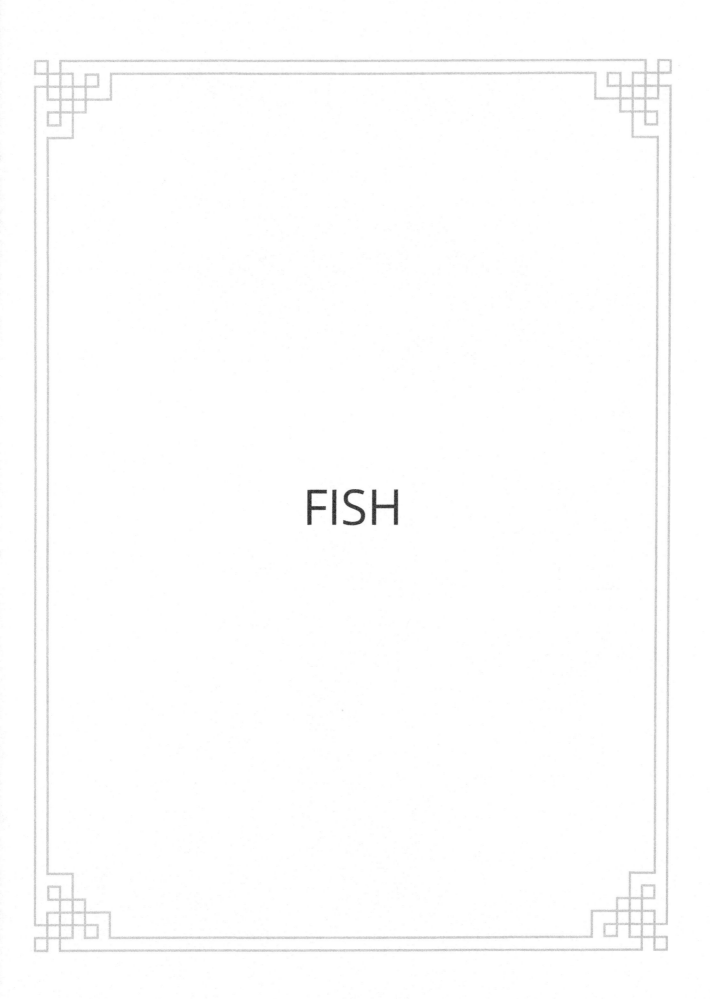

FISH

Servings: 2

Calories: 563

Ready in 25 min

SALMON ON FENNEL

Ingredients:

1 red onion,

2 fennel tubers

2 or 3 tomatoes

2 thyme branches

2 tbsp walnut kernels

4 tbsp olive oil

salt

pepper cayenne

2 fillets of salmon

2 tsp provençal herbs

approx 180 mg purine

Instructions:

Peel the onion and cut it in half before slicing it into strips. Fennel should be cleaned and washed before removing the stalk, halving, and cutting into strips. Tomatoes should be cleaned, washed, and chopped. Pick the leaves off the thyme after it has been washed and dried. Chop the walnut kernels coarsely. Heat 2 tbsps of oil in a pan and cook the onion strips and fennel for 5 minutes over medium heat. Sauté for another 5 minutes with the nuts and tomatoes, add 2 tbsps of water and cook for another 5 minutes over low heat, sealed. Season with salt, pepper, thyme, and cayenne pepper to taste. Clean the salmon fillets by rinsing them, patting them dry, and seasoning them with salt. In a separate pan, heat the remaining oil and fry the salmon fillets for 3 minutes on both sides over medium heat, seasoning with herbs de Provence, salt, and pepper. On top of the vegetables, place the salmon fillet.

STEAMED SNAPPA

Ingredients:

½ cup of okra washed and trimmed

1 cup pumpkin peeled and cubed

4 medium snapper fish or another white fish on your choice

2 cloves of garlic crushed

1 onion thinly sliced

1 chopped tomato

½ tsp coarse black pepper

1 tsp ground coriander

1 bay leaf

2 whole pimentos

2 sprigs of thyme

scotch bonnet pepper

approx 170 mg purine

Instructions:

Season the fish with the scotch bonnet, garlic, black pepper, bay leaf, ground coriander, and thyme. This can be done in advance and left to marinate in the fridge overnight. Add the vegetables and a little water to a non-stick pan and heat gently for 5-7 minutes, then place the marinated fish on top of the vegetables and cover with a tight-fitting lid.

Simmer on low heat for 20 minutes or until the fish is cooked all the way through. Serve with boiled yams or plain rice and vegetables of your choice.

Servings 1

Calories: 937

Ready in 20 min

AVOCADO LIME SALMON

Ingredients:

6 oz skinless salmon(170 g)
1 clove garlic, minced
olive oil, to taste
salt, to taste
pepper, to taste
½ tsp paprika
for avocado topping:
1 avocado, chopped
¼ red onion, chopped
1 tbsp fresh cilantro, chopped
1 tbsp olive oil
salt, to taste, pepper, to taste
1 tbsp lime juice
approx 300 mg purine

Instructions:

Preheat the oven to 400°F (200°C).
Line a baking sheet with parchment
paper.
Rub the salmon with garlic, olive
oil, salt, pepper, and paprika on the
prepared baking sheet.
Bake for 10-12 minutes, until soft.
Make the avocado topping: In a
small bowl, gently mix the avocado,
red onion, cilantro, olive oil, salt,
pepper, and lime juice. Don't
overmix, or you'll break down the
avocado.
Spoon the avocado topping over the
salmon.

SOLE IN OVEN

Ingredients:

4 fillets of sole fish
2 tbsp of olive oil
1 handful of parsley
1 tbsp of thyme,
1 sprig of rosemary
1 tbsp of marjoram
salt and pepper
2 cloves of garlic
juice of one lemon
1 lemon
approx 150 mg purine

Instructions:

Chop the garlic and parsley, add salt and pepper, marjoram, thyme. Put everything in a large dish with lemon juice and olive oil. Dip the fillets in the sauce on both sides and arrange them on a baking dish. Cut the lemon into wedges and dispose of them over the fillets. Add more parsley if you want. Bake in a preheated oven at 356F/180C for 20 minutes. Serve on a hot plate.

Servings: 4

Calories: 120

Ready in 25 min

BOILED SOLE

Ingredients:

4 fillets of sole
water
1 bunch parsley
1 bay leaf
1 tbsp of olive oil
coarse salt
lemon
approx 150 mg purine

Instructions:

Immerse the sole fillets in boiling water with parsley, bay leaf, extra virgin olive oil, and salt; then let it boil for about 15 minutes.
Drain them, put them on a plate, and season with oil, a little salt, and lemon.

MACKEREL WITH GREEN SAUCE

Ingredients:

1 medium-sized fresh mackerel
1 iceberg lettuce leaf
salt
black pepper
olive oil
1 clove garlic
1 handful of fresh parsley
lemon in juice
approx 160 mg purine

Instructions:

In a low and large pan, boil two fingers of water and add the whole mackerel, cover with the lid and let it cook 4/5 minutes. Turn off and let it cool.

For the green sauce: In a blender, mix the iceberg leaf, one tbsp water, and salt.

In a small bowl, prepare a sauce with oil, chopped parsley, quartered garlic, salt, black pepper, and a few drops of lemon. Arrange the mackerel steaks on a plate and season well with the sauce from a small bowl. Pour the green sauce into a single-portion glass bowl and place them next to the mackerel.

Servings: 4

Calories: 140

Ready in 20 min

COD IN WHITE SAUCE

Ingredients:

4 cod fillets

5 tbsp of flour

olive oil

1 clove of garlic

1 lemon

2 tbsp of capers

10 olives

a handful of fresh parsley chopped

approx 130 mg purine

Instructions:

Flour the filets on both sides. Heat a little oil with a clove of garlic and brown it, careful not to burn the garlic.

Remove the garlic. Place the fish in the pan and fry them on both sides to take on a nice golden color.

Deglaze with the juice of a lemon, grate a little lemon peel, add capers and olives, and cook, taking care to keep the cod well moist and covered with the sauce.

Cover so that the sauce does not dry out too much, wait another minute or two and serve with fresh parsley.

Printed in Great Britain
by Amazon

24129676R00086